Other books by the authors of *Miracle of Life*

BY ROBERT G. WELLS, M.D., AND MARY C. WELLS
Menopause and Mid-Life

BY KEN GIRE
Intimate Moments with the Savior
Incredible Moments with the Savior
Instructive Moments with the Savior
A Father's Gift
When You Can't Come Back
(with Jan and Dave Dravecky)

BY JUDY GIRE
A Boy and His Baseball

Devotions for Expectant Mothers

Miracle of Life

ROBERT G. WELLS, M.D, AND KEN GIRE
MARY C. WELLS AND JUDY GIRE

WITH PHOTOGRAPHS BY LENNART NILSSON

ZondervanPublishingHouse
Grand Rapids, Michigan

A Division of HarperCollinsPublishers

For all my obstetrical patients who have for years
granted me a matchless privilege, sharing with them one of life's
most exhilarating experiences, the births of their babies.
    DR. ROBERT G. WELLS

For my mother, Lois, and my grandmother, Lydia . . . because they prayed.
    KEN GIRE

Special thanks to Wendy Peterson for her assistance
in distilling the research and for her creative input into the project.
    ALL THE AUTHORS

    ❧

Miracle of Life
Copyright © 1993 by Robert G. Wells and Ken Gire

Requests for information should be addressed to:
Zondervan Publishing House
Grand Rapids, Michigan 49530

Published in association with the literary agency
of Sealy M. Yates and Associates, Orange, California.

The photographs in this book are reprinted with the permission of the
photographer, Lennart Nilsson, and are taken from *A Child Is Born* by Lennart
Nilsson, published by Dell Publishing Company; and from *Being Born* by Sheila
Kitzinger and Lennart Nilsson, published by the Putnam Publishing Group.
Used with permission. All rights reserved.

The quotations from *A Time to Be Born* by Julie Martin are reprinted with permission
of Thomas Nelson, Inc. The quotations from *The Prophet* by Kahlil Gibran and
The Velveteen Rabbit by Margery Williams are reprinted with the permission of
Alfred A. Knopf, Inc.

Cover design by Jack Foster Design
Cover calligraphy by Timothy R. Botts
Interior design by Gary Gnidovic/Doug Johnson

Printed in Mexico

96 97 / DR / 10 9 8 7 6 5 4 3

*I*T WAS SAINT AUGUSTINE who said: "We take for granted the slow miracles whereby year by year water irrigating a vineyard becomes wine; we stand amazed when the same process takes place in quick motion in Cana of Galilee."

What is taking place within the well-irrigated vineyard of your womb is a miracle, but it happens so slowly we take it for granted. After all, nine months is a long time to wait for a miracle.

During those nine months God is not only preparing a baby for the parents, he is preparing the parents for a baby. So much has to be rearranged to accommodate this new life—not just making room in your home but making room in your heart.

And that takes time.

God could have performed the miracle in "quick motion," and it would have turned everybody's head; but he chose to do it slowly, content to turn only yours.

Of course, some of the brimming wonder will spill over to your husband, just as Mary's wonder spilled over to Joseph. But it was she who felt the flutter of the Christ-child within, she who nourished the fragile life, she who pondered the miracle in her heart. To Joseph it was given only to feel the child's movements from the outside, only to nourish the child's mother, only to be midwife to the miracle.

For nine months your husband will know this child only from afar, but you will know it from deep within you. For within you it will live and move and grow. What you eat, it will eat. Where you go, it will go. For nine months you will be one with this miracle.

As the miracle grows, you will undoubtedly have concerns about its development. To address some of your physical concerns we have included a weekly progress report that will help you understand what is going on inside your womb. To address some of your spiritual concerns we have provided a devotional section consisting of a passage of Scripture or a quotation, followed by a prayer.

"More things are wrought by prayer than this world dreams of," wrote the poet Tennyson. And there is no more important task you could commit yourself to than praying for your unborn child. Current research indicates that the unborn child senses whether or not it is wanted long before birth. And what better way is there to communicate your longing for that child than by consistently praying for it? As you do, you will notice that the prayers in this book are unfinished. That is because they are merely a springboard to get you started on more specific prayers of your own.

After each prayer is a place where you can journal some of your own thoughts and feelings and prayers. This section will become a written record of your pregnancy so that later you can take it down from the shelf, dust off its pages, and relive some of the memories. Someday you will want to share those memories with your child. Sharing your thoughts during the pregnancy and the details of the birth is an important way to communicate to your child that it was wanted and welcomed into the world as a special human being. And someday, when your child is grown and married and nurturing a miracle of its own, you may want to pass this book on as a keepsake.

Will your child be a blue-jeaned, barefoot boy with baseball on his mind? Or a rosy-cheeked girl with a mind full of make-believe and dress-up and tea parties on the back lawn?

Since only God knows at this point, we thought it helpful to alternate genders throughout the book to make the prayers more personal. Should you learn your baby's sex during the course of your pregnancy, simply make the shift in your mind as you read and pray.

And since you would have consulted a book like this only after you had learned you were pregnant, we have summarized what has taken place inside you up to that point. Thereafter we follow your pregnancy week by week.

The weeks should coincide with your doctor's calculations for how far along you are. There are two ways of determining this. One is gestational age; the other is fertilization age. Gestational age starts with the time of your last menstrual period; fertilization age starts at conception when the sperm enters the egg, which is about two weeks later.

Most physicians date the pregnancy by gestational age. The reason is simple. Usually women don't know when they conceived, but they do know when they had their last period. Since pregnancy lasts about 280 days or 40 weeks from a woman's last menstrual period, that has become a fairly standard way of arriving at a due date.

Lastly, through the in utero photography of Lennart Nilsson, you will peer into the womb itself. The procedure is performed with an instrument called a fetoscope. Only a few millimeters in diameter and equipped with a wide-angled lens, the fetoscope is inserted near the woman's navel while she is under general anesthesia, although in many cases only a local anesthetic is used.

Great care is taken so as not to injure the baby and so you can witness this miracle of life—this slow miracle that is transforming the water in your womb into the wine of a wonderful human being.

Behold, children are a gift of the Lord;
the fruit of the womb is a reward.
PSALM 127:3 (NASB)

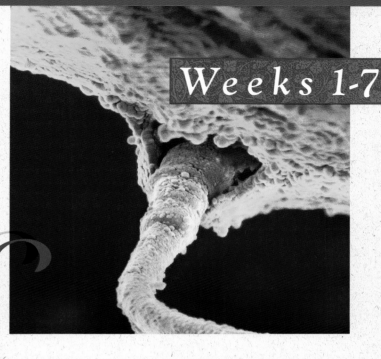

So, YOU'VE JUST returned from the doctor's office where your suspicions have been confirmed. You're pregnant! ❧ Congratulations! ❧ The nausea, the tender breasts, the fatigue, those unsuspected mood swings—they weren't all in your mind after all. ❧ Since you were probably about seven weeks along when you saw your doctor, you must be wondering what's been going on inside you all this time. Well, it started about two weeks after your last period. That's when you ovulated, when a ripe egg called an ovum burst forth from your ovary. At that time the egg was smaller than the dot on an i.

*T*his barely visible egg then began drifting through one of your Fallopian tubes, the two five-inch tubes that link your ovaries to your uterus. Lining the Fallopian tubes are thousands of hair-like projections, something like swaying kelp on the ocean floor, which slowly swept the egg along on its journey.

While you and your husband were resting in each other's arms, as many as five hundred million of his sperm were teeming inside your vagina in a frenetic search for that egg. Shaped like microscopic tadpoles, the sperm lashed their whiplike tails to squirm through the small opening in the lower part of your uterus called the cervix. From there they wriggled upstream into the uterine cavity and then out into the many folds and recesses of the Fallopian tubes. By the time they reached the egg, only a few hundred survived the rigorous swim.

*W*hen the first sperm located the egg, it plunged headlong into it with reckless abandon. Then the chemical composition of the egg's wall changed, hardening to prevent any others from entering. Once inside, the winning sperm shed its tail and burrowed its head deeper into the egg, where it united its nucleus with the nucleus of the egg.

That is when the miracle of life began. Twenty-three chromosomes of your husband's sperm melded with twenty-three chromosomes of your egg to form your baby's unique set of genetic blueprints. Whether your baby will be a boy or girl, tall or short, have your eyes or your husband's smile or grandma's dimples is all determined by the genes in that dowry of forty-six chromosomes.

As the cells divided, they continued to be swept downstream through the Fallopian tube until, about the fourth day after fertilization, they finally reached the uterus. For a couple of days this raspberry-shaped cluster of cells floated in the nourishing fluids there. Then it nested in the thick, spongy lining of the uterine wall. A few days later it sank its roots and began drawing its nourishment from the blood vessels in the lining of the uterus.

*D*uring the fourth gestational week (two weeks after fertilization) the cells in the cluster formed specialized layers. Then one set of cells formed a bubble of salty liquid called the amniotic sac, which encased the burgeoning cells to cushion them. Another set of cells developed into the yolk sac to manufacture blood for the emerging embryo. Still another set grew to become the placenta, its fray of fleshy strands braiding your baby to your body. Each beat of your heart pumps blood to the placenta, through the umbilical cord, and into your baby's bloodstream, feeding it with oxygen and nutrients.

By the fifth gestational week, your baby's primitive heart began to beat. About that time you were probably beginning to suspect you were pregnant. Your period was late. Your breasts were getting larger. Your bladder was getting smaller. And you were so tired. So very, very tired.

By six weeks your baby had gone from a single cell to an embryo, ten thousand times larger than that fertilized egg, or about the size of an apple seed.

The heart was pumping newly formed blood throughout the baby at a rate of sixty-five beats a minute—the same heart that would one day pound on Christmas morning, sink at bedtime, and break after a summer romance. By the seventh week the embryo has budded with rudimentary arms and legs, which are ridged, indicating where the fingers and toes will be. From the sixth to the seventh week the embryo has grown from the size of an apple seed to the size and shape of a black-eyed pea. Already it has nostrils, lips, a tongue, and even nubs where teeth will one day grow.

Amazing, isn't it? All that growth and development in just seven short weeks.

No wonder you were so tired!

i've been waiting for you now
no more wondering about me—
whether or not this miracle of life
would ever happen inside me

now i can wonder about you—
about what color threads
He's weaving you with

brown eyes or blue
will you like to swim or draw
bake bread or engineer buildings
will you throw your head back
    and laugh hard
    or just grin

i don't know
i don't know

but i do know that i will
    love to hear you call my name
i will love to feel your tiny
    hand in mine
i will love to watch your tummy
    rise and fall
    in sweet sleep

and i know that sometimes you
    will hate me
sometimes you will shrink from
    my touch
sometimes your fevered breathing
    will rattle my soul
    in the dark dark night

but until then
please baby grow strong
take all you can from me please

until then
i'll be waiting for you

JULIE MARTIN
A Time to Be Born

Dear Lord,

HIS IS A PRAYER unlike any I have ever prayed. A life is growing inside me, a life that the world has never seen before and will never see again. A sacred life. Thank you so much for allowing me to share in this miracle. The very thought of it fills me with joy and wonder. I am humbled by the honor, and I feel most blessed.

But I also feel most unprepared. So much needs to happen in my life before I will become the mother this child deserves.

Strengthen my arms so they can shelter this little one from life's storms. Soften my hands so they can bring comfort in life's rejection. Broaden my shoulders so they can be climbed on when he's feeling playful, leaned on when he's feeling tired, cried on when he's feeling sad or hurt or discouraged. Enlarge my heart so I can rejoice with him in his triumphs and weep with him in his defeats.

I commit myself to this child all the days of my life. Please take from me to provide for his nourishment. Please watch over the formation of every cell and bring him into this world whole and healthy.

I commit this child to you, Lord. I take comfort in knowing that you are his true parent and I, only his guardian. Help me to guard him well. And to guide him well.

Guide me well, too, Lord, for little feet will follow in my steps. Guide my eyes so I would look to you to show the way and to set the pace.

Give me the grace to be patient as this miracle of life unfolds within me, and the perseverance to pray so I may play an even greater part in its unfolding. . . .

_____

_____

_____

_____

_____

_____

_____

_____

_____

_____

_____

_____

_____

_____

_____

_____

_____

_____

_____

_____

_____

_____

_____

_____

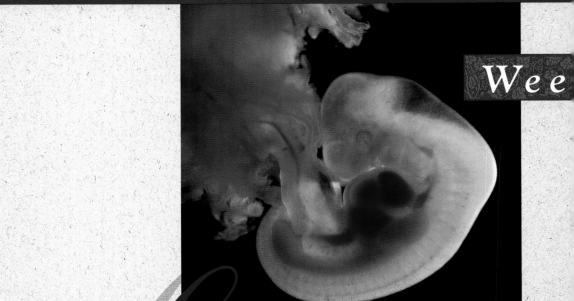

*L*IKE A LUMP OF KNEADED clay in the hands of a great sculptor, your baby's features are beginning to take shape. Every curve, every indentation, is being molded by the same artist who fashioned the universe. Though the little lump of flesh he is working with is only about the size of a lima bean, it already has distinct detail. Your baby's dark eyes are no more than indentations in her skull, yet tiny eyelids are already being formed to cover them. The tip of the nose snubs out from the

8

emerging face, and the ears are being molded with great care.

A little farther down, the faint beginnings of ribs look as though the sculptor's hand has brushed softly across a torso of clay. Your baby's legs are lengthening from the Creator's gentle pull, and her arms are curving chestward as if to protect her heart. Through the transparent skin shimmers a spinal cord, growing so fast it causes the baby to be hunched over. Elbows that will one day get scraped on the playground are being fashioned without the slightest imperfection. Knees that will one day get skinned on the sidewalk are being rounded as smoothly as the finish on a porcelain doll. Fingers and toes that were last week only nubs are now being shaped as delicately as ceramic flowers.

Internally, the major organs are all in place, though not fully developed. The most developed organ is the baby's heart, which beats 140 to 150 times a minute—twice as fast as your own—keeping the clay of your baby's flesh moist and pliable.

This little lump of clay is God's magnum opus, his great work of art, fashioned in his image, after his own likeness. And he has chosen your womb as his workshop.

> **B**efore I formed
> you in the womb I
> knew you, before you
> were born
> I set you apart.
>
>
>
> JEREMIAH 1:5

Dear Lord,

HANK YOU for how you are fashioning my baby's joints, shaping her face, smoothing her skin. I marvel at the way you work, so patient in your artistry, so painstaking in your attention to detail. Swaddled within the folds of my womb lies a baby I haven't seen or heard or touched, yet I long to know her.

In my longing, help me to realize that you long for her too; that you are the one who knew her first, and loved her first; that she was conceived in your mind before she was ever conceived in my body; that she was set apart not to fulfill my will but yours.

Help her to grow up pliable to that will, Lord, responsive to every touch of your hand upon her life. Shape within her a spirit so sensitive to spiritual things that she will be able to feel your breath when you whisper to her conscience, sense your shadow when you move across the circumstances of her life.

Use this little life to mold me, Lord. Use her clinging fingers to make me more gentle and her sudden smile to make me more joyful. Use her countless spills to make me more patient and her helpless cries to make me more compassionate. Use her to mold me not only into more of a mother but more of a human being. . . .

A Journal of My Thoughts, Feelings, and Prayers

*Y*OUR BABY is now about the size of a grape and is in the latter stage of his embryonic development, which lasts from week five through week ten. This is a critical time as the embryo is especially vulnerable. ❧ Toxic substances you ingest such as drugs and alcohol can have a particularly detrimental effect on your baby during this time. Diseases such as rubella (German measles) can cause anatomical defects in the baby's organs, heart problems, deafness, even cataracts. And unshielded X-rays can cause brain damage. You may already be having some fears about these things—fears you hesitate to think about, let alone express. Is my baby healthy? Will he be normal? Will he have all his arms and legs? Will he be all right mentally? Will he be premature and have to spend his first months in an incubator? Will he be forced to live with some debilitating illness I could have prevented? Those fears are completely natural; all women experience them at some time during their pregnancy. But, in reality, only about three percent of babies are born with major defects. And many of those could have been prevented with proper prenatal care. So, although you need to be careful during this stage in your baby's development, you need not be fearful, as long as you're under the care of a competent physician and are following his advice.

One reason to allay those fears is because of the strategic role the placenta plays in protecting your baby. The placenta encases the embryo and anchors it to your uterus, where tiny blood vessels from both you and your baby intertwine. As a result, oxygen and nutrients are filtered to your baby, while harmful substances are filtered out—much the same way a coffee filter allows water to pass through but not the grounds. Some medications, though, can pass through the placenta and harm your baby. That's why it is so important to inform your physician of any medications you may be taking. As your baby's heart beats, the waste products in his blood pass to your blood supply for disposal. So the placenta allows your baby to be nourished and cleansed at the same time, all the while keeping your blood supplies distinct. They are so distinct you may even have completely different blood types.

Another function of the placenta is to pass antibodies on to your baby. This provides him with a certain level of immunity until he starts producing antibodies of his own, sometime around six months after he is born.

With the formation of the placenta God has cupped his hands around your little one so that he will be cushioned, nourished, cleansed, and protected from disease and infection. So don't feel bad about having a few fears; just don't let them haunt you. And don't let them overshadow him who has provided this ever-present refuge for your baby's protection.

> **G**od is our refuge and strength, an ever-present help in trouble. Therefore we will not fear, though the earth give way and the mountains fall into the heart of the sea, though its waters roar and foam and the mountains quake with their surging. . . . The Lord Almighty is with us; the God of Jacob is our fortress. . . . "Be still, and know that I am God."
>
>
>
> PSALM 46:1–3, 7, 10

P

Dear Lord,

LEASE WATCH OVER MY SON. He is so tiny and so vulnerable, especially at this critical time in his development. Keep him safe and warm and well-nourished. Keep him free from disease and deformity and disability.

I pray for a strong baby, Lord. A strong, healthy baby. A baby who can hear lullabies and see pictures in storybooks. A baby who can grow up to run and chase puppies and play hide-and-seek with the kids in the neighborhood.

I am asking as a mother, Lord, and on behalf of someone too small and too weak to ask for himself.

You who were a friend to the weak, please befriend my baby during this critical time. You who were so kind to children, please be kind to this child of mine. You who would not break off a bruised reed or extinguish a dimly burning wick, please protect this frail little life that flickers within me.

And when my fears get the better of me, help me to be still and know that you are God—my refuge, my strength, my ever-present help in trouble. . . .

*A*T THE TENTH WEEK your uterus is about the size of a plump peach; and your baby, about the size of a small apricot. ❧ This is an important week, marking your baby's transition from being an embryo (literally, "one teeming with life within") to a fetus (literally, "young one"). The fetal period is a time of rapid growth. ❧ It is also a time when bone cells make their first appearance, a natural marker signaling that the internal structure of your baby is all in place. A beating heart. A functioning brain. Two kidneys. Stomach. Intestines. Pancreas. Liver. All the organs are there, awaiting a more permanent skeleton to encase them. ❧ Although your baby's skeletal structure was complete by the eighth week, it was made entirely of cartilage, the gristle that makes up your ears and the tip of your nose. This week the flexible cartilage

O

is being replaced by bone to create a sturdier, more protective framework for your baby. Your baby's jaw, shoulders, arms, and legs are all undergoing the magical transformation. But though we know something of the mechanics of this process, much of it remains shrouded in mystery.

*I*ncredibly, in just fifty or so days your baby has gone from a single cell to millions of cells, all of them programmed for specialized and highly complex tasks.

> **A**s you do not know the path of the wind, or how the body is formed in a mother's womb, so you cannot understand the work of God, the Maker of all things.
>
> ECCLESIASTES 11:5

At three weeks after conception two pulsating tubes came together to form a heart. What secret message was scrawled within their genes to tell them what to do, how to do it, and when?

At the same time a complex network of nerves emerged to integrate and coordinate all the bodily functions. How did they know where to lay the lines, where to connect them, and how?

A short time later a head bulged out of nowhere to house this central command system. Arms and legs appeared, as if suddenly summoned to life. Organs, elbows, and eyes, everything burst into existence as if the Creation were being reenacted within you. What word spoke the cells into existence? What command separated them?

What a mystery hovers over the dark, primordial waters of your womb!

WHAT IS GOING ON INSIDE ME is such a mystery. I am awed at how each cell responds to its genetic instructions. A gene says to one cell, "Make a heart," and it makes a heart. Another gene says to another cell, "Make bone," and it makes bone. It's all so mysterious to me how those genes give their orders, and equally mysterious how the cells obey them.

Help me to obey you like that, Lord. Help me to be as obedient to your Word as those cells are to the encoded information on those genes.

Help me to realize that just as those cells are genetically coded to produce a human being, so I have been genetically coded by my new birth to become conformed to the image of your son.

Just as I don't know how my child is being formed within my body, so I cannot understand how your son is being formed in my soul. But I thank you that I too am your workmanship, and that you, the Maker of all things, are forming him within me.

Shape me into his image, Lord, so that when I cradle my baby in my arms she will see something of the eyes of Jesus when I look at her, hear something of his voice when I talk, feel something of his gentleness when I hold her.

As she grows up, may she see in me glimpses of his love, his understanding, his tenderness. Help me to become such a compelling likeness that she would naturally be drawn to him, drawn to know him, to love him, trust him, obey him.

*W*hat a glorious hope you have placed in my heart—Christ in me—a mystery even more awe-inspiring than the one within my womb. I pray that someday you will place this same mystery in my daughter's heart so that one day she will be able to show Jesus to her little child. . . .

~ A Journal of My Thoughts, Feelings, and Prayers ~

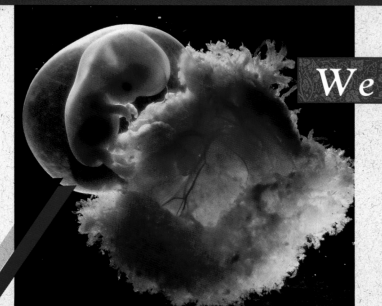

*Y*OUR BABY HAS NOW GROWN to about two inches in length. His head, which accounts for half of your baby's size, is upheld by a slender neck, which is now strong enough to raise the chin off his chest. Within this developing neck are the vocal cords, readying themselves for that first shivering cry at birth. 🙠 If you could pull the covers back and peek inside the cushioned darkness of your womb, you would be able to see the external genitalia budding between your baby's legs. 🙠 You would also be able to notice your baby inhaling and exhaling, swallowing gulps of amniotic fluid. You might think he would drown with all that fluid passing down his throat and into his primitive lungs, but remember, your baby gets his oxygen not from breathing but from the blood that passes through the umbilical cord.

In the next three weeks your baby's length will double, as his trunk and extremities are going through a growth spurt to catch up with its still disproportionately large head. With only seven months until delivery, your baby still has a lot of work to do before he can move out of the soft cradle within your womb and into the nursery you are getting ready within your home.

So expect to let your waistline out a little more and to feel a lot more tired.

> *P*arents are often so busy with the physical rearing of children that they miss the glory of parenthood, just as the grandeur of the trees is lost when raking leaves.
>
>
>
> MARCELENE COX

Dear Lord,

SOMETIMES IT SEEMS there is just so much that needs to be done to get ready for this child. So much to plan and prepare for. Getting the nursery in order. Rearranging the furniture. And I want to give the house a good cleaning, because I know there won't be time for it after the baby comes.

But, Lord, I continue to be so tired. Will I be this tired after the baby comes? Will I have enough energy to do all a mother needs to do? To wash all the clothes that need to be washed, cook all the meals that need to be cooked, clean up all the messes that need to be cleaned up? And aside from all those domestic needs, Lord, what about the needs of my baby? Will I have enough energy to read all the storybooks that yearn to be read, answer all the questions that hope to be answered, play all the games that want to be played?

Don't let all that needs to be done overwhelm me, Lord. And don't let parenthood become just another household chore. The glory of being a parent is there now. Help it to be there when my baby is two, and ten, and thirteen going on eighteen.

And years from now when I'm picking up toys and towels and casually discarded old socks, help me not to be just bent over, raking leaves. Help me to see the branching grandeur of the tree you entrusted to my care—the tree I first loved when it was smaller than an acorn. . . .

AT YOUR THREE-MONTH CHECK-UP you will probably get to hear your baby's heartbeat. This is done with an ultrasound machine called a *Doppler device.* The rhythms you hear will be rapid, almost as if your little girl has been searching for you these past twelve weeks and is now running to your arms. As you bend down to scoop her up, she throws her arms around your neck, clutching your head against her chest, and in the embrace you hear her racing heart. That heart began to form during the fifth week of your pregnancy or just three weeks after conception. At that time two tiny tubes joined together, which later bulged into four chambers. The two top chambers are the atria; the two lower ones, the ventricles. By the seventh gestational week a dividing partition of tissue separated the right atrium from the left. At the same time the ventricles developed a muscular partition that separated them. Openings between the chambers were also formed, and shortly afterward, the valves that regulate blood flow.

> **A**bove all else,
> guard your heart, for
> it is the wellspring
> of life.
>
>
>
> PROVERBS 4:23

As your baby's heart developed, so did the system needed to support it. From the placenta, oxygen-rich blood flows through the umbilical cord to feed your baby, and once inside its body this blood travels to the fetal heart. There it is pumped to the brain and to the rest of the body.

Since the lungs have not yet expanded and are unable to produce oxygen, they are bypassed. At birth your baby will have to adapt quickly, going from total dependence on you for her oxygen supply to being totally on her own.

How this happens is a small miracle in itself. But that miracle is a long way off; the closer miracle is the heart of a little girl racing to her mother. And if you listen carefully, you can hear the mother's heart racing to meet her.

T

D e a r   L o r d,

HANK YOU FOR THE BEAUTIFUL MOMENT in the doctor's office when that whooshing heartbeat first introduced me to my daughter. Already I love her, Lord. Already I want to hold her, to feel her panting heart against mine as she gropes to nurse and learns to draw life from me all over again.

Guard that little heart, Lord. It is so fragile and it races so fast. Keep it healthy and beating strong.

Guard her spiritual heart too. Keep it pure and free from pollution. Keep it fresh and flowing and free from stagnation. Above all else, keep it in love with you.

Give her a heart with great room in it, Lord; a heart full of kindness and tenderness and compassion; a heart whose door is always open to those who need shelter from whatever storms may have swept across their lives.

Should that heart ever grow weary, bring her to your feet where she can find rest; should it ever grow troubled, lead her to green pastures where she can find peace; and should it ever grow cold, take her in your arms so the warmth of your embrace can melt her heart and once again start it beating for you. . . .

*D*URING THE PAST couple of weeks the connections have greatly increased between your baby's nerves and muscles. Your son has been trying out those muscles, going through all sorts of sudden, marionette-like move-ments—flexing his arms, rotating his wrists, bending his knees, turning his feet, curling his toes. ❧ By this week your baby's muscles have grown more substantial and his movements more deliberate. He swims in a heated pool of amniotic fluid, his buoyant twists and turns looking like the graceful move-ments of some Olympic swimmer.

As he moves about, his thumb will occasionally brush against his lips, prompting his head to turn and find it. When it does, his mouth will instinc-tively take the thumb and begin sucking. At birth your baby will be rather unceremoniously evicted from the only home he has ever known, and sucking his thumb is his way of preparing for that day when he must grope for his food.

On that day the soft warmth of your womb will be replaced by the coarse rub of cloth against his skin, by the drafty chill of air around his face. The secure darkness he is used to will give way to the unrelenting glare of hospital lights. The calming rhythm of your heart will be replaced by the discordant bustle of medical routine. And no longer continu-ously fed by the umbilical cord, your baby will experience strange sharp pains he has never felt before—the pangs of hunger.

In his piercing hunger he will cry out for the satisfying warmth of your milk.

And in his shivering aloneness he will cry out for the soothing comfort of your presence. For from your breast he not only will receive the milk he needs for his body, but the milk he needs for his soul—the milk of maternal compassion.

> Can a mother forget the baby at her breast and have no compassion on the child she has borne?
>
> Though she may forget, I will not forget you!
>
>
>
> ISAIAH 49:15

Dear Lord,

HANK YOU that you have stooped to use the quiet, gentle image of a mother nursing her baby to describe the feelings you have for your children.

That one image communicates so much to me, for I know even now that there is no way I could ever forget this baby who will nurse at my breast. My compassion flows out to him as freely as the milk from my breast. And if that's true, Lord, how much more does the milk of divine compassion flow out to your children. Especially when they cry out in the middle of the night, pierced with hunger, alone and scared and shivering in the dark.

Lord, when I cry out to you in my emptiness, help me to realize that you have not forgotten me; when I cry out in my aloneness, help me to understand that you have not forsaken me.

Through my tears, help me to see that you are there, aching with maternal feelings, longing to take me in your arms where the milk of your compassion will be my food; the softness of your breast, my pillow; and the rhythms of your heart, the lullaby that sings me to sleep.

It is such a beautiful image you have chosen, Lord. Bring it to mind every time I nurse. And keep it in my mind all the days of my life. For one day I too may be shivering in the dark, feeling empty and alone, and desperately needing the comfort of your breast. . . .

A Journal of My Thoughts, Feelings, and Prayers

THE FOURTEENTH WEEK marks the beginning of the second trimester, a time when your baby's skeletal cartilage begins ossifying into bone. The ribs and vertebrae have already begun to harden, even though your baby is only about four inches long and weighs barely an ounce. ❧ You can rest a little more comfortably during the beginning of this trimester as your morning sickness has probably abated if not ended altogether. Your mind can also rest a little easier because the risk of developing congenital defects is, for the most part, behind her.

This is because all her organs are now fully formed and functioning. The digestive system is able to contract and push food through its bowels. The gall bladder is already producing bile to aid in digestion. Meanwhile, the pancreas is busy making the insulin that will burn excess sugar in your baby's body when she's had too much cotton candy at the circus or too much ice cream while running errands with Grandpa. The pituitary gland is beginning to produce hormones that will further stimulate growth and development, hormones that will one day lead your daughter across the threshold of adolescence into adulthood.

That nostalgic song about children growing up is all too true: "Turn around and she's two . . . turn around and she's four . . . turn around and she's a big girl, walking out of the door."

Fortunately, that day is a long way off. The only threshold she's crossing this week is the one leading to her second trimester.

But already, as she crosses it, she looks somehow older. Her head is rounder and more distinctively human. Her eyes, which started out on the side of the head, have moved closer together. And the eyelids, though sealed, can squint. Your baby can make all sorts of facial expressions. She smiles and frowns and when lightly brushed on the forehead even turns her head away.

It's unmistakable now—your little girl is growing up.

> Before becoming a mother I had a hundred theories on how to bring up children. Now I have seven children and only one theory: love them, especially when they least deserve to be loved.
>
>
>
> KATE SAMPERI

Dear Lord,

SOMETIMES I FEEL SO INADEQUATE to raise this child. When I browse through the bookstores at all the advice on raising children, I am overwhelmed at how much I don't know. Help me to benefit from the insight and experience of others. But help me to realize that if I read all the books and implement all the theories yet do not have love, it profits me nothing. And profits my child even less.

Help me to love my child, even at those times when she least deserves it. Especially at those times, Lord. For isn't that the way you loved us? When we were yet sinners. When our faces were frowning and turned away from the light of truth. When we least deserved it.

Give me a love that will cover the multitude of sins my daughter will commit in her childhood; and give her a love that will cover the multitude of sins I will commit in my adulthood. Give me a love that will overlook her childish behavior; and give her a love that will overlook mine. For there are times I, too, whine when I'm hungry, get exasperated when I'm hot, and throw tantrums when I'm tired.

But I seem to be getting tired a lot less these days, and I thank you for that, Lord. I thank you also for how quickly my baby is developing. For an eagerly expecting mother, she can't grow fast enough. But I know there will be a day when I won't want her to grow anymore. For I know that if she keeps growing, one day I will turn around and she will be gone.

That will be a sad day. When it comes, Lord, slip a little picture in her heart. Some tattered, play-worn memory of a mother who once loved her as a little girl.

And who loves her still. . . .

A Journal of My Thoughts, Feelings, and Prayers

_____

_____

_____

_____

_____

_____

_____

_____

_____

_____

_____

_____

_____

_____

_____

_____

_____

_____

_____

_____

_____

_____

*I*S IT A BOY OR A GIRL?"
This is probably the most common question
an obstetrician is asked. During the first
months of your pregnancy your baby's sex can't be
determined by simply looking at the developing
embryo, because boys and girls start out looking the
same. ❧ The actual process of differentiating the male from the female
is accomplished by hormones. As rising sap causes a tree to bud in
early spring, so fetal hormones cause the sexual budding that is taking
place between your baby's limbs. ❧ It is not until the eleventh week

that the sexual organs begin to bloom. In both boys and girls, a small bud burgeons between the legs, with two swellings on either side of it. In boys, the bud will develop into a penis, and the swellings will grow together to form the sack-like scrotum. In girls, the bud will develop into a clitoris; below it a slit will form the opening of what will become the vagina; and the swellings on either side, which formed the scrotum in the male, will form the labia.

A microscopic inspection of the baby's sexual organs reveals remarkable development. In the ducts of the boy's testicles the precursors to sperm have already formed. And in the girl's ovaries five million follicles have already formed, each containing an ovum. So, if you're carrying a girl, she will already have her lifetime endowment of eggs.

> **C**hristian marital love is (or should be) as close as we are likely to experience to being "a piece of Heaven on earth," for it is a true leftover from Paradise.
>
>
>
> MIKE MASON
> *The Mystery of Marriage*

Although physical distinctions aren't visible to the naked eye until the second trimester, the sex of your baby is determined at conception. Your egg and your husband's sperm each contain twenty-three chromosomes, one of which is a sex chromosome.

The sex chromosome can be either an X or Y chromosome, X being female and Y being male. Your egg always has an X chromosome; your husband's sperm may either have an X or Y. If the sperm uniting with the egg is a Y chromosome, the resultant pair will be XY. And since the male chromosome is dominant, the baby will be a boy. But if the sperm's sex chromosome is an X, the resultant pairing is XX, and your baby will be a girl.

The differences between the sexes is by divine design that dates all the way back to the Garden of Eden, where "male and female he created them." And that design not only makes the mandate to "be fruitful and multiply" possible, but immensely pleasurable.

Dear Lord,

GIVE ME THE WISDOM, I pray, to know what to tell my son about sex. Give us such an open relationship that he would not be shy in asking questions and that I would not be self-conscious in answering them.

Help me to teach him to respect his sexuality as one of the many wonderful gifts you have given him, a gift that he will one day share with the woman he loves.

Thank you, Lord, for another one of your gifts, the gift of marital love.

Thank you for the sweet pleasures within its garden and the secure feeling within its walls.

Help him to understand that through marital love he can experience something of the Paradise that was lost in Eden. Help him also to understand that even in the most pristine of Paradises things can go wrong when the boundaries you have established are disregarded. Help me to explain why those boundaries are there—not to keep him from tasting those pleasures, but to enable him to enjoy them to the fullest.

Help me to teach my child about this wonderful garden. And may the strongest lessons come by way of example, by the tender and loving way his father and I have cultivated our love for each other. . . .

ALTHOUGH NOBODY really believes boys are made of snips and snails and puppy dog tails any more than they believe girls are made of sugar and spice and everything nice, most people do think there are fundamental differences between the sexes. ⁊ Aside from the obvious anatomical differences between boys and girls, many see differences in the way they perceive the world, in the things that capture their imaginations, and in the way they interact socially. ⁊ Many studies have been conducted to account for these differences. Some researchers lean on the nature side of the debate, concluding the differences are biologically determined. Others lean on the nurture side, concluding they are behaviorally determined. A more balanced approach suggests both play a major role. Though more research is needed, the studies that have been done are intriguing, especially those dealing with the fetal brain. ⁊ Early in its formation the brain divides into two hemispheres. The right side processes visual and spatial information;

therefore it is more artistic and musical. The left processes language and thought; therefore it is more analytical and critical.

In girls, the left hemisphere develops earlier than in boys; consequently, so does their verbal ability. In boys, the right side develops earlier; consequently, so does their visual and spatial ability.

The two sides of the brain are linked by the *corpus callosum,* which is something like a telephone cable with a thick bundle of fibers that sends information back and forth between the hemispheres. The girl's link between the hemispheres is larger and wider than the boy's and therefore allows for a freer flow of information. This anatomical difference between the sexes can be seen during the fetal stage of development. Since communication between both sides of the brain is essential in reading, this may explain why, on a whole, it's easier for girls to learn to read than boys.

Current research indicates that the male and female brains are not only different structurally but chemically. The male sex hormone testosterone causes boys to be more aggressive. Girls, on the other hand, have a higher level of the neurotransmitter *serotonin,* which has a calming effect on behavior and probably quells any aggressive tendencies. So chemicals are at least partly responsible for why boys play rougher than girls, why they like more action-oriented stories, and, as they get older, why they are more aggressive sexually.

Though differences exist between boys and girls, they should not be exaggerated to obscure the differences between individual children, which are often more distinct. To see those differences in your children is one of the primary tasks of parenting, because those differences will affect every area of your relationship with them, from how you discipline them to how you direct them in their vocation.

> Seeing begins with respect. There are as many ways to learn, I suppose, as there are ways to see, but it is clear that no one can truly see something he has not respected.
>
>
>
> STEVEN J. MEYERS
> *On Seeing Nature*

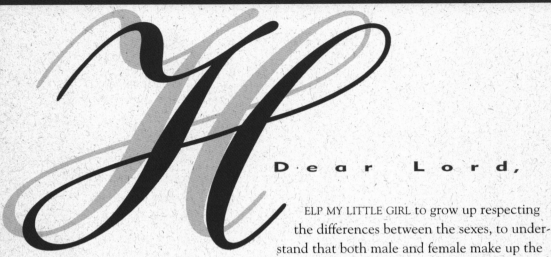

Dear Lord,

ELP MY LITTLE GIRL to grow up respecting the differences between the sexes, to understand that both male and female make up the image of God. Help her to appreciate her femaleness and the unique way she was created, not only as a woman but as a human being.

Help her to feel special about the unique set of eyes she was given to see the world around her, and the unique mind she was given to understand that world and the unending variety of people within it.

Help her to see that diversity is God's way of making the world a more beautiful place to live. How pretty the daisy is with its white petals radiating so symmetrically from its golden center; yet how monotonous the world would be if all the flowers in all the meadows had white petals radiating symmetrically from golden centers. How impoverished the world would be without its blushing roses and its shy morning glories and its speckled fields of wildflowers.

Help her to grow up seeing that each person belongs here, that each person has a place in this world. May she grow up respecting that place, Lord. And may she learn to walk gently through life so as not to trample the wonderful variety of people who are struggling to grow.

And, Lord, help me not to trample on this child of mine who will also struggle to find her place in the world. Help me not to expect her to be just like me, to think like I think or to feel like I feel. Give me the grace to accept the fact that we may not like the same music or the same styles in clothes, that we may not have the same goals or the same dreams. Help me to value those differences in her, Lord, and to nurture them so she may grow up to become everything you hoped she would. . . .

A Journal of My Thoughts, Feelings, and Prayers

_____

_____

_____

_____

_____

_____

_____

_____

_____

_____

_____

_____

_____

_____

_____

_____

_____

_____

_____

_____

_____

_____

_____

_____

_____

THE FETAL WEIGHT HAS DOUBLED in just two short weeks, and your baby now weighs about three-and-a-half ounces. He is just beginning to react to the sounds within and without your womb, as his ears are formed and functioning. ❧ The next time you're taking a bath, slip underwater and listen to the sounds around you. You'll find yourself in a world of drips and bubbles and gurgles, as the nearer sounds are all amplified. The sounds you hear may be a little indistinct because of air pockets trapped in your ear canals. Your baby lives in a world surrounded by the steady swish of your heart, the empty growl of your stomach, and the digestive gurgles of your intestines, but since he has no air in his ears and since water conducts sound better than air, the sounds he hears are more distinct.

If you would have someone call to you from the next room while you were submerged in the tub, you would hear something of what your baby hears from outside the womb. Layers of muscle and fat dull the sound by about thirty decibels, but the melody of the voice comes through without distortion, almost like hearing music in the distance but not being able to understand the lyrics.

A recent experiment in Ireland underscored the effect of sound on the unborn. The theme song to a popular soap opera was played repeatedly to babies in the womb who were only thirty weeks old. After they were born the theme song was played again, and suddenly they became alert and attentive!

> Recently, for my weekly newspaper column, I invited seventy-five fourth and fifth graders to submit the words they most like to hear from their mothers. Here are the five big winners, repeated over and over by almost all kids:
> I love you. Yes. Time to eat.
> You can go. You can stay up late.
>
>
>
> DOLORES CURRAN
> *Traits of a Healthy Family*

Dear Lord,

THIS NEW LIFE IS GROWING UP SO FAST. I can hardly believe my little boy can already hear. I guess that means now I not only have to watch what I put into my mouth but what comes out of it as well.

I pray that the sounds my baby hears coming out of my mouth are pleasant ones. May he hear laughter and songs and words that are kind, instead of yelling and grumbling and words that are harsh. Help me now, Lord, even before he is born, to create a peaceful environment for him.

After he is born, may the rhythms of my voice soothe him and comfort him and make him feel welcome in the foreign world he has entered. And when he is older, may I still have a voice that soothes and comforts and welcomes. For the world is full of things that will startle him, scare him, and make him feel like a stranger—from the first time he falls on his face when learning to walk to the tenth time he falls on the sidewalk when learning to ride his bike. For those traumatic times and for all the times in between, may I be the one he runs to. And when I warn him to be careful, may the teaching of kindness be on my lips and the tone of kindness be in my voice.

Help me also, Lord, to learn to hear him, to listen to all that he says, especially to the unspoken things he says that are so important for a mother to understand, like the wordless feelings that will brim in his eyes or the inarticulate reactions that will wash over his face. Help me to understand the language of his heart, Lord. And help him to understand mine.

Help me to be a mother whose tone of voice is music to a child's ear. I pray you would give me a voice that would have a "yes" in it as much as is possible. Keep me from becoming a mother who is always saying "no," a mother who protects too much, restricts too much, worries too much.

As he grows up, may the most favorite words he hears from me be, "I love you." May he never out-grow his joy in hearing those words, and may I never out-grow my joy in saying them. . . .

*T*HE EMBRYO STARTS MOVING as early as the eighth week. It's not much more than a twitch of primitive reflexes or a flutter of nerve impulses, but it marks the beginning of your baby's activity. At the end of the first trimester, as the nerve fibers became connected to the muscles, that activity increased. The twitches became stretching movements, and the flutters turned into pirouettes. ✤ Until now these warm-up exercises have taken place in the quiet, sequestered gymnasium of your womb. But over the next few weeks that will all change. Maybe it already has. Maybe you felt something inside you, something as soft as the tiptoeing of ballet shoes. That something was your little ballerina making her debut, stepping out onto the stage and dancing her way into your heart.

Now you can only sense the sweep of her hand across your womb or the flutter of her feet as she leaps, but soon you will be able to learn all the subtle nuances of movement. Soon you will be able to tell when your baby is asleep, when she is awake, and when she is warming up for her next performance.

Enjoy the ballet while you can. In a few months that petite, five-ounce ballerina will

> My heart is not proud, O Lord, my eyes are not haughty; I do not concern myself with great matters or things too wonderful for me. But I have stilled and quieted my soul; like a weaned child with its mother, like a weaned child is my soul within me.
>
> PSALM 131:1–2

become a five-pound kick-boxer, punching out your ribs and wheeling around to kick your bladder! In a few months more she'll be out of your womb and into the world, an active little newborn. Before you know it, she'll be scooting around on the carpet to explore the house, then teetering on her feet to discover the yard, and then toddling all over to take on the world.

Dear Lord,

IT WAS SO EXCITING TO feel my baby moving, that soft sensation as she brushed up against me. I tingled with all the excitement of a little girl who longingly touches the lacy hem of the store-window doll she wants for Christmas. I can't wait to feel it again, Lord, that sensation of her life brushing so softly against mine. I can't wait to hold her in my arms. To feed her. To dress her. To tell her stories and sing her songs and play peek-a-boo.

There are so many things I want her to experience in life. So many books I want her to read. So many activities I want her to be involved in—ballet classes and piano lessons and art projects.

I'll be a proud mother, Lord. Proud of every picture she draws, every mud pie she makes, every dusty thing she brings me from under the couch.

But, Lord, don't let her ever think that what she does is why I love her; don't let her think that she has to excel at some activity to gain my acceptance, my affection, my approval.

Help her to realize that a mother's most satisfying moments are not seeing her child involved with great matters, whether that's excelling at school or on stage. A mother's most satisfying moments are when her child, no longer needing the milk from her breast, crawls onto her lap, to rest in her arms, stilled and quieted by the familiar rhythms of her heart.

Through my maternal feelings for this child, help me to understand what I can do to bring the most satisfaction to you, Lord. May my soul be like a weaned child within me, stilled as it rests in your lap and quieted as it is rocked by the gentle rhythms of your heart. . . .

*I*F YOU COULD PEER into the womb, you would see scarlet strands of blood vessels woven just beneath your baby's sheer, silken skin. The embroidery work is so intricate the naked eye cannot even see the finer threads of capillaries that transport the life-giving blood to every cell. So small are some of the capillaries that the blood cells must travel single file to get through them. ❧ Even more intricate is your baby's nervous system. Like the capillaries, the delicate stitches that attach nerves to muscles are invisible to the naked eye. The weaving of this network of nerves began as early as eighteen days after conception, and it won't end until several weeks after your baby is born. ❧ The completion of the nervous system takes this long because each stitch must be made with meticulous care, as all of the other bodily systems are largely integrated and coordinated by the nervous system. ❧ For example, take the simple act of hearing a lullaby. To pick up all the subtle variations of sound, your baby will need more than 240,000 hearing units, which will be coordinated by approximately 100,000 nerve cells. Given the dimensions of the inner ear, the needlework will have to be done with painstaking skill and precision.

And how about the simple act of smelling the subtle fragrance of baby powder? More than twelve million nerve endings will be needed within the nose for him to accomplish that small feat. And for him to take in the bright colors of a storybook, more than fifty billion light-sensitive points within the retina of the eye will be needed.

The invisible network of nerves will allow him not only to delight in the taste of chocolate chip cookies hot out of the oven, but it will also protect him from that oven by causing his hand to recoil in pain if he reaches out to touch it before it cools.

> **F**or you created my inmost being; you knit me together in my mother's womb. I praise you because I am fearfully and wonderfully made; your works are wonderful, I know that full well. My frame was not hidden from you when I was made in the secret place. When I was woven together in the depths of the earth, your eyes saw my unformed body. All the days ordained for me were written in your book before one of them came to be.
>
> PSALM 139:13–16

Dear Lord,

I AM AMAZED HOW YOU can knit together the intricate network of nerves that someday will sense every sharp corner of furniture, every playful tickle of a father's fingers, every tender stroke of a mother's hand. When my boy takes his first step, it will be because of the nerves you connected to his legs and coordinated with the rest of his body. When he says his first word, it will be because of the complicated stitchwork lining the tongue and vocal cords with nerves that will carry the commands from the brain and form them into sounds. When he smiles at me for the first time, it will be because you have sewn those muscles around his mouth with such painstaking care. Thank you for all my baby will be able to do because of how carefully you are weaving him in my womb.

Thank you for both the pleasures he will enjoy and the pain he will have to endure. For the times he will skip down the sidewalk, and for the times on that same sidewalk when he will skin his knee and come home crying for me to kiss away the pain. For the honey and the bee stings. For the home runs and the strike outs. For the laughter and the tears. For all the variegated threads of experience that will make up the tapestry of his life, I thank you, O Lord.

I pray it's a long one.

But however long a life you have measured out for my little boy, please make it one that is beautiful, and meaningful, and that somehow, in some way, gives honor to your name. . . .

A Journal of My Thoughts, Feelings, and Prayers

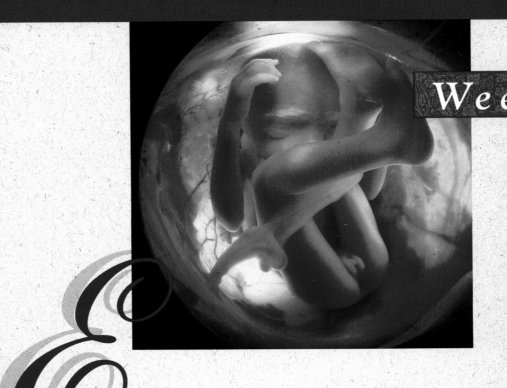

*E*ARLY IN THE EMBRYONIC development only one layer of cells stretched to cover your baby. As the cells differentiated themselves, this one layer split into two: the *dermis*, or inner layer, and the *epidermis*, or outer layer. By the twentieth week the epidermis has become further differentiated into four layers. ❧ The whorled ridges on the hands and feet comprise the outermost layer, making gripping easier for the hands and traction easier for the feet. It also is responsible for fingerprints, another evidence of your baby's unique place in the world.

The inner layer of skin is where fat is stored, where the sweat and oil glands are forming, and where the hair is rooted. Your baby already has a downy coat of hair called *lanugo* (from the Latin word for "wool"), but soon that will be replaced by the developing hair follicles.

Somewhere around this week your baby will start secreting a white, greasy substance—something like shortening—which mixes with the dead skin cells that are shed, forming what is called the *vernix* (from the Latin word for "varnish").

The vernix clings to the fine lanugo, which is concentrated on the baby's head. Before birth the lanugo is shed, but there is still enough vernix clinging to the head so that when the baby's head engages in the birth canal, it will be easier for it to squeeze through the constricted opening. The vernix also acts as a protective ointment for your baby's delicate skin to guard against infection and from becoming wrinkled or adversely affected by the salty amniotic fluid.

When I was a child, I enjoyed observing sea anemones on the California coast.

They were often found in tidal pools among the rocks. About four or five inches in diameter, they look like colorful flowers with soft, wavy tentacles.

But I noticed an interesting phenomenon. Sometimes I'd take a stick and poke one of them. Immediately the sea anemone would withdraw its sensitive tentacles and close up until it became a shell. It was similar to a beautiful flower closing. Now it was protected from further injury.

What happens with the sea anemone illustrates what happens to a person when he is offended. The tentacles of that sea anemone are similar to the spirit of a person. The sea anemone is completely open and vulnerable. But when the stick pokes him, he closes up.

GARY SMALLEY
The Key to Your Child's Heart

Dear Lord,

OW FRAGILE is this little life within me. Her fingers and toes sway in the salty pool of the amnion just like the tentacles of a sea anemone swaying in a tide pool on the seashore. Her see-through skin stretches so delicately over her internal organs and shields her so protectively.

I know all that will change before birth. The skin will thicken. The pigments will darken. And someday there will be calluses from running barefoot through the summer months. But even then, Lord, help me to realize that, no matter how tough it appears, the skin of another human being is a delicate thing.

Help me to treat this child tenderly, Lord. Not simply because her skin is delicate, but because the spirit beneath that skin is delicate too. It is sensitive and can be easily hurt. Protect that tender spirit of hers, Lord.

Keep my words from poking her. Keep my humor from thrusting a stick into an area that is sensitive. Keep my correction from becoming a painful jab of ridicule. Keep her from having to withdraw into a shell to protect herself from me, Lord. Instead, give me the resolve now, even before she is born, to lay down the verbal sticks and stones that might hurt her and cause her to become closed. . . .

A Journal of My Thoughts, Feelings, and Prayers

_____

_____

_____

_____

_____

_____

_____

_____

_____

_____

_____

_____

_____

_____

_____

_____

_____

_____

_____

_____

_____

_____

_____

_____

_____

THE SONOGRAM will be the first pictures you see of your baby. The pictures are created from inaudible, high-pitched sound waves that are directed at your baby through a device called a *transducer*. The transducer is swept slowly across your abdomen, which has been slathered with gel or mineral oil to improve the transducer's contact with the skin. ✍ The sound waves bounce off of the tissues and back to the transducer, something like sonar looking for a submarine. In fact, it was for anti-submarine warfare during World War II that this technology was first used. These sound echoes are then converted to images that you will see on a monitor. Since tissues of different density reflect sound differently, bone tissue will show up more distinctly than the tissue, say, of less dense organs like the liver or kidneys. ✍ During the ultrasound, measurements will be taken of your baby and the rhythms of his heart will be carefully monitored. A thorough scanning will be done of everything in the uterus to assure that everything is properly formed and functioning. If your doctor does several sonograms over a period of time, it can be determined whether the baby is growing at a healthy rate, and it can even be roughly estimated how much the baby will weigh when he's born. The ultrasound equipment also allows the doctor to tell the age of your baby—and whether you have one or two or three of them tumbling around inside you!

Besides all this, the ultrasound is good at detective work, helping to determine whether there are any abnormalities in the baby. The machine can also detect abnormalities in the mother, such as uterine tumors. Other clues, such as the amount of amniotic fluid, help the doctor deduce whether the baby is in any kind of danger.

Unlike X-rays, ultrasound sends no harmful radiation through your baby's body; and unlike amniocentesis, the procedure is noninvasive. There is no discomfort, except for an extremely full bladder from the several glasses of water you have to drink beforehand. The full bladder serves as a landmark so the doctor can locate the other pelvic organs, and it enables the transducer to display clearer images on the monitor.

But don't expect these images to be anything you can enter in some "cutest baby contest." Do expect, though, to be overwhelmed as you are given your first glimpse into the miracle of life growing within you.

> The sonogram. We are about to snatch a glimpse of the miracle of life. Do we dare?
>
> Lying on the cool vinyl table, I look over my shoulder at the black screen. The doctor flips on the switch. An image appears....
>
> And I wonder if God allowed the angels to watch Him form Adam from the dust.
>
>
>
> JULIE MARTIN
> *A Time to Be Born*

Dear Lord,

THANK YOU for drawing the curtain and allowing me to take a peek at this miracle of life in the making. It was a sacred moment, I think, that angels must long to see.

Even if it was only a sound echo, only a chalk drawing on a dusty blackboard, it was still wonderful. That distinctly round head. That tiny throbbing heart. That grainy gray silhouette. Even swaddled in so much darkness, that scruffy little boy of mine was beautiful.

What a wonder it was to see him. Floating there. Paddling around like some carefree kid in a vinyl backyard pool. Thrashing in the water. Oblivious to the eyes that watched . . . or to the stir he created in our hearts.

Thank you that I will be giving birth to this beautiful baby at a time when medical technology has made so many advances. Only a century ago things were so primitive and mortality rates were so high for both the mother and her baby.

Especially, Lord, thank you for my doctor. For all the time he spent in school, and for all the sacrifices he made to get that education. For the risks he took to get his practice started, and for the long hours he puts in to take care of the patients who need him, of which I am only one.

Thank you, too, for all the sacrifices his wife has made. For her patience all those times his beeper went off and interfered with their plans together. She is a special woman, and I pray you would honor her for all of those sacrifices.

Thank you, too, for his family, and for their being so unselfish with him, and for understanding the demands his unique profession requires of him.

Bless him, Lord. Give him the strength to do all that he has to do, and the rest he needs so that tomorrow he has the strength to do it all again.

And somehow, Lord, give him back some of that precious time he missed with his wife and family. . . .

A GENERATION AGO, the first twelve years of life were considered the most formative in a child's development. The last wave of research suggested that the most formative time is the first three years of life. Current research pushes back that time to include life within the womb. ❧ That's right. During the nine-month term in your womb, your baby is not only developing physically but intellectually as well. And who is the renowned doctor responsible for these revolutionary findings? ❧ None other than Dr. Seuss! ❧ A study was conducted with a group of sixteen mothers in the last six-and-a-half weeks of their pregnancies where twice a day they read Dr. Seuss' book *The Cat in the Hat* aloud to their babies. After the babies were born, the doctors conducting the study monitored their sucking patterns. When they played a tape recording of the mothers reading the story, they noted the pattern, labeling it "Pattern A." When they played a tape of the mothers reading a poem titled "The King, the Mice and the Cheese," they noticed the babies altered their sucking patterns, which the doctors labeled "Pattern B."

People were also bringing babies to Jesus to have him touch them. When the disciples saw this, they rebuked them. But Jesus called the children to him and said, "Let the little children come to me, and do not hinder them, for the kingdom of God belongs to such as these."

LUKE 18:15–16

*A*t only three-days old, fifteen out of the sixteen babies altered their sucking patterns to make the tape machine switch to *The Cat in the Hat*. It was not the content of the story the babies wanted to hear, but the cadences of the sentence structure, the familiar rhythms that to them were so soothing to hear. From those findings we know that your baby is not just cuddled away in your womb, listening, but she is learning as well.

Just like a little toddler, isn't it? Begging mother to read her favorite story over and over and over again.

D e a r L o r d,

T IS SO EASY TO OVERLOOK little children by thinking that all they can understand are simple words and nursery rhymes. But if it is true that they start learning in the womb, then it's never too early to teach them about you—which is probably why those people brought their babies to Jesus.

To be sure, they wanted his blessing on their children. But maybe there was something else. Maybe they wanted their children to have the experience of being able to sit on his knee and gaze into his eyes, to gather around him and hear the gentle words that fell from his lips.

How many of those children grew up remembering that morning when they huddled at his feet? Maybe they didn't remember his words any more than the babies in that study remembered the words to *The Cat in the Hat*. But maybe there was something beyond words that they understood.

Help me to see, Lord, that the children brought to Jesus were not too young to comprehend the look of love in his eyes or the sound of kindness on his lips. May my little girl see that look in my eyes and hear that sound on my lips, so that when she crawls down from my lap she might feel as if she has sensed in a small way or for a small moment something of your presence. . . .

A Journal of My Thoughts, Feelings, and Prayers

*T*HERE IS SOMETHING else your baby learns in the womb. Something infinitely more important than distinguishing the patterns of speech in a storybook. Researchers have discovered that the womb is not only where the first stirrings of intellectual development take place, it is also where your baby's emotional development begins. ❧ Early in its fetal development your baby begins to hear. Somewhere between the twentieth and twenty-fifth week, your son's hearing is comparable to an adult's. To a certain extent, the noises your baby hears for the remainder of your pregnancy will help form his early impressions of the world he is about to enter. Whether he hears peaceful words or verbal tirades will make a difference in how secure your baby will feel coming into that world.

Is it a safe place? Or is it filled with danger? Is it an ordered place? Or is it filled with chaos? Is it a relaxing place? Or is it filled with anxiety?

Researchers say that by the sixth month your baby leads an active emotional life and is even able to discern your moods and attitudes. Loud, discordant sounds can cause him to flinch and recoil.

Also, high levels of stress you feel are distilled into chemicals that can be transmitted through the placenta where they are absorbed into your baby's bloodstream. If the stress is sustained over long periods of time, it is suspected, though not conclusively proven, that it not only affects your baby's emotional well-being but possibly even his physical and mental development.

This second trimester is a good time for you to focus on the world you are bringing your baby into, to make sure it's a place that is safe, secure, and soothing.

It is also a time to focus on your own feelings. Studies indicate that even in the womb the baby may be able to perceive the mother's overall feeling toward him. Probably the best thing you can do for your baby now is to make him feel wanted, something he will need to feel from you all his life if he is to grow up into an emotionally healthy person.

> If you make children happy now, you will make them happy twenty years hence by the memory of it.
>
>
>
> KATE DOUGLAS WIGGIN

I Dear Lord,

WANT THIS LITTLE BOY to know how much I love him. I want him to know how much joy he has brought to my life. I realize, Lord, that he won't understand these things, at least, not fully, until someday when he has children of his own. But, Lord, help him even now to understand this: help him to know how much he is wanted.

Help me to show him how much. By the sparkle of delight in my eyes when I smile at him. By how quick I am to drop a mother's chores and play with him. By the unhurried way I read him stories, even stories I've read to him a hundred times before. Especially those stories, Lord, because they will create such a vivid memory for him.

Help me to give this boy a happy childhood, filled with late nights and pillow fights and stories read by flashlight under his covers. May his mornings be filled with building forts, his noons with peanut butter sandwiches eaten in a tree house, and his afternoons with baseball with the neighbor kids.

May his childhood be filled with such happy times, Lord, that when he looks back on them, twenty, thirty, forty years hence, the memories will bring a smile to his face and a reassurance to his heart that he was wanted, and that he was loved. . . .

Y OUR BABY WEIGHS a little more than a pound. The face is fully formed. The eyelids are no longer fused, yet remain closed until this, the sixth month, when the eye completes its development. ❧ Your baby's body is becoming more proportionate and more straight, having grown out of the curled, fetal position she has been in since her early development. The stretching takes place in a supple sac surrounding your baby called the *amnion*. The outer membrane of the amnion is made up of tough but elastic tissue, so there's no danger of your baby stretching too hard or kicking a foot and poking a hole through it. ❧ The word *amnion* comes from a Greek term meaning "little lamb," so named because when lambs are born, they are enclosed in a similar protective bubble. Like a shepherd carrying a little lamb in his arms, this sac of warm water cushions your baby from all the jolts and jostles that will come her way during the course of the pregnancy. It also exerts a constant pressure on the uterus to keep it expanding so it can accommodate your baby's growth.

The surface of the amnion is glazed by a single layer of cells that is constantly growing, allowing the bubble to expand and keep pace with the baby. With its spherical shape and opalescent sheen the amnion resembles a transparent pearl.

Sometimes the fluid within the amnion looks cloudy because fetal cells, lanugo hair, and vernix have shed and are floating in it. But even with the baby's urine flowing into it, the amniotic fluid is sterile. A big reason why is that the fluid is continually being renewed. About one-third of it is removed and replaced every hour, amounting to a six-gallon exchange each day.

Aside from cushioning your baby from any sudden impact, the amnion regulates the temperature of the water surrounding your baby, keeping it a constant 99.5 degrees Fahrenheit. This helps guard against infection by discouraging the growth of certain kinds of bacteria. With the amnion wrapped so warmly and so securely around her, you can rest assured that your little lamb is in good hands.

> He
> tends
> his flock
> like a shepherd:
> He gathers the lambs
> in his arms
> and carries them
> close to his heart;
> He gently leads
> those that have
> young.
>
> ISAIAH 40:11

Dear Lord,

HANK YOU FOR GATHERING my little lamb in your arms and carrying her close to your heart. I feel so secure knowing she is nestled there. Thank you for leading her beside the still waters of the amnion, for the nourishment she receives there, the warmth, the protection. Thank you for the way you shepherd your flock, not only for your strength in carrying the weak, but for your sensitivity in leading the weary. Thank you that you not only have compassion for the little lambs but for the mothers who bear them.

Thank you for the gentle way you have led me on this slow, plodding, uphill trail to motherhood. You could have driven me. You could have left me straggling behind. But you did neither. You slowed your pace that I might walk beside you.

Whatever valleys I have to walk through during this pregnancy, however dark, however deep, however depressing or discouraging, I will fear no evil, for Thou, O Shepherd, art with me. . . .

YOUR BABY NOW WEIGHS around a pound and a half, the heaviest single feature being the skull. Unlike the rest of the skeleton, which began with cartilage, the skull begins with five distinct plates that emerge from the base of the skull. ❧ These plates are something like the tectonic plates under the earth's crust. And like fissures in the earth's crust, narrow spaces exist between these plates, exposing the tough membrane surrounding the brain. These spaces are called *sutures*. They're called that because they look as if they have been sewn together with stitches. ❧ The design is an engineering marvel as these plates move and may even slightly overlap each other as the head makes its way through the birth canal. Were it not for this unique design, it would be almost impossible for the head of a large baby to pass through the birth canal.

Fortunately, and this is the real marvel, the reshaping of the baby's head does not damage its brain. A couple of days after the baby is born, the plates move back together, and the head regains its normal shape.

As you stroke the top of your newborn's head, you may become alarmed that the middle has a "soft spot." This is the place where the sutures come together. If you place your fingers over these sutures, you will be able to feel blood pulsing through them.

For that reason the sutures are also called *fontanels*, a term that means "little fountains." These little fountains do a big job, irrigating the soft spots with blood to speed up the fusing of the plates. And when they do finally fuse, sometime between the first year and a year-and-a-half of your baby's life, that built-in crash helmet will be ready to protect him as he starts taking those tentative first steps around the house.

> **S**uccessful parenting means: One, becoming what you should be. And two, staying close enough to the children for it to rub off.
>
>
>
> ANNE ORTLUND
> *Disciplines of the Home*

Dear Lord,

I AM AMAZED at the provision you have made to protect my baby's life during childbirth. How precisely you have designed this miniature human being. Everything is engineered so intricately and works so perfectly. It's all so incredible.

But, Lord, where are the instructions?

Where are the things I need to know to raise this boy into a man? What curriculum do I use to ensure that he will learn all you want him to learn? What school do I enroll him in so he can become everything you want him to be?

Help me to realize, Lord, that my heart will be the place where this child goes to school; and my life will supply some of the books he will study to learn how to grow up.

But what will my son learn in that school and from those books? What lessons will he pick up from watching me when he looks up at me with those big bright eyes of his? What words will he learn to speak? And how will he speak them? What things will he learn to do, or to neglect? What skills will he learn from the habits of my life?

Help me to become what I should be, Lord, and to stay close enough to this child for it to rub off.

Help me to be a good teacher, long on patience and short on lectures. And may my principles be like the plates in my baby's head, firmly in place and yet flexible enough to allow him to make it through the many difficult passages he must travel on his way to becoming a man. . . .

A Journal of My Thoughts, Feelings, and Prayers

*T*HE BABY'S GOSSAMER SKIN is becoming more opaque now, almost as if the body were becoming self-conscious about its mysteries. The weight of these combined mysteries is almost two pounds, and the length of them from head to toe is around fourteen inches. ᑇ The thickening of the skin prepares the way for a veritable forest of hair follicles, along with wells that will provide the necessary oil and water for the skin's maintenance. Each square inch of skin will eventually contain seven hundred sweat glands, one hundred oil glands, and a labyrinth of some twenty-one thousand nerve cells that will sense the softest breeze blowing across your baby's crib or the smallest pin pricking against

6

her foot.

With the second trimester drawing to a close, your baby's lungs pass through an important step in their development. Cells inside the lungs begin to manufacture a fatty substance called *surfactant*. This substance keeps the air sacs in your baby's lungs partially inflated after she takes her first breath. Without it, the lungs would collapse.

*Y*our doctor no longer has to use a Doppler device to pick up the baby's heartbeat because the heart is stronger now, and a special stethoscope is all that's necessary. During the remaining months your doctor will monitor your health as well as the health of your baby. With each checkup, each blood test, each pelvic exam, each sonogram, you will learn more about your baby and how she is developing. It will be only the beginning of all that God has to teach you through the gentle life of this little child.

*A*t that time the disciples came to Jesus and asked, "Who is the greatest in the kingdom of heaven?"

He called a little child and had him stand among them. And he said: "I tell you the truth, unless you change and become like little children, you will never enter the kingdom of heaven. Therefore, whoever humbles himself like this child is the greatest in the kingdom of heaven."

MATTHEW 18:1–4

Dear Lord,

KNOW I HAVE much to teach this child, from teaching her how to tie her shoes to looking both ways before crossing the street to putting her hand in yours so someday she can walk with you.

But I also know I have much to learn from this child.

Help me never to forget that, Lord. Teach me the gentle lessons from her life.

Teach me from the simple and honest way she prays.

Teach me from the trusting way she clings to my hand, confident that I will guide her when she walks and steady her when she stumbles.

Teach me from the innocent way she explores the world around her, from the eager and uncomplicated way she receives a gift, and from the sweet and unselfish way she gives one away.

Teach me from the instinctive way she runs to me when she's hurt or crawls in bed with me at night when she's scared of the thunder or afraid of the dark.

Teach me from the uninhibited way she plays and from the contented way she rests on my lap when she's too tired to play anymore.

*L*ord, I know there will be times I have to tell her no and she won't understand why. Help me to learn there will be times like that for me as well. Times when you say no to my desperate pleas. Times when I must trust that you have my best interests at heart, however unaware I may be as to what those are.

Teach me what it means to become like a child. Give me the humility to learn from someone so much smaller, so much weaker, and so much less knowledgeable than myself. And grant me the wisdom to understand that weakness has lessons that strength cannot teach. . . .

*T*HIS WEEK MARKS the beginning of the third trimester, the final term before your baby graduates to life outside the secure walls of your uterus. He now weighs around two pounds and is about fifteen inches long. ❧ Your baby is becoming more and more sensitive to your movement. When you move, your baby curls up. When you rest, he gets active. Almost as if reaching out to explore the world around him, your baby will grasp the umbilical cord when he bumps into it. And to get a good look at that world, this month he will open his eyes, staring and blinking like the suddenly-opened eyes of a newborn puppy. ❧ Your baby's eyes first start developing about the fifth week of pregnancy. Initially, the primitive brain sends out two hollow tubes, each of which forms a small sphere on the end. At about eight weeks blood vessels thread their way to the eye, and by the next week the pupil forms. During this time the neurological connections between the eye and the brain develop, forming the optic nerve, which will take the raw sensory data collected by the eye and send it to the brain for processing. In the weeks that follow the cells of the eye will differentiate themselves into the lens, the cornea, and the iris. The last thing to form is the protective sheath of skin that will be the eyelid.

Since light is diffused through the skin, the view from the womb is probably, at its brightest, a dim orange glow. How much a baby can see in the womb is uncertain, but we do know, through an intrauterine exploratory procedure called *fetoscopy,* that when babies see light they turn away and shield their eyes from it with their hands.

> If a child is to keep alive this inborn sense of wonder... he needs the companionship of at least one adult who can share it, rediscovering with him the joy, excitement and mystery of the world we live in.
>
>
>
> RACHEL CARSON
> *The Sense of Wonder*

The eyes are only receptors; the brain is the interpreter. It sorts the sensory information it receives, setting up a filing system of images that it will draw upon for the rest of your baby's life.

Your little boy will learn most quickly from the images he is repeatedly exposed to. That's why he will respond favorably to your face, which will be familiar to him, but may recoil at the face of a stranger, whose features will be foreign and difficult to interpret.

At birth, your baby will only be able to focus his eyes at a distance of one foot—just the right distance so when you hold him in your arms he will be able to see you. And what he sees will be the first wonder he encounters in a world that will be to him so full of so many wonderful things.

Dear Lord,

ELP ME TO INSTILL within my child a sense of wonder so indestructible it would be able to weather whatever disillusionment he may encounter on the road to growing up. Help me to realize that instilling my child with this sense of wonder is more important than good posture or athletics or proper grammar. Remind me of that often, Lord, for I know I will often forget. As we walk hand in hand together, may this little child lead me back to the fields of my own childhood, to the fascination of dandelions puffed into the air, of butterflies flitting from flower to flower, of rainbows hung out to dry.

Thank you, Lord, that through him I am given another chance at life, another chance to lie on my back and point out faces in the clouds, another chance to skip flat rocks across smooth ponds, another chance to see the world reborn, and for me to be reborn along with it. . . .

~ A Journal of My Thoughts, Feelings, and Prayers ~

_____

_____

_____

_____

_____

_____

_____

_____

_____

_____

_____

_____

_____

_____

_____

_____

_____

_____

_____

_____

_____

_____

_____

_____

*I*N THE LAST FOUR WEEKS your baby's weight has doubled. She now weighs some-where around two-and-a-half pounds. After the twenty-eighth week the baby is considered viable, that is, capable of living outside the womb. Although with recent advances in medical technology, prema-ture babies weighing much less than this are surviving now. ❧ For most of your baby's development the head has been disproportionately large in relation to the rest of the body. Now all that has changed, as over the past few weeks the head has been catching up. ❧ Within that head is a complex brain, which began to form around the fourth week of your pregnancy. By the seventh week, nerve cells connected with each other to form pathways where electrical impulses shuttle information to and from the brain with lightning speed.

One hundred thousand of these nerve cells are created every minute. By the time the baby is born, the number of nerve cells will reach one hundred billion, and the number of connections between those cells will reach ten trillion. So massive is this maze of wiring that all the telephone lines in the world would be only a fraction of the total network needed for all the communication that is processed by your baby's brain.

The fetal brain is divided into two hemispheres, which have remained smooth-surfaced until this week. Now it has begun to wrinkle, forming its characteristic grooves and indentations, making room for the accompanying increase in brain tissue. Interestingly enough, every normal human brain has these grooves and indentations in exactly the same place and to exactly the same depth.

Your baby's brain is an incredible mechanism. One day it will be able to scrapbook her childhood experiences so that even very late in life something as slight as the musty smell of an attic can bring back a flood of memories.

> [The mind] may be likened to a garden, which may be intelligently cultivated or allowed to run wild; but whether cultivated or neglected, it must, and will, bring forth. If no useful seeds are put into it, then an abundance of useless weed seeds will fall therein, and will continue to produce their kind.
>
>
>
> JAMES ALLEN
> *As a Man Thinketh*

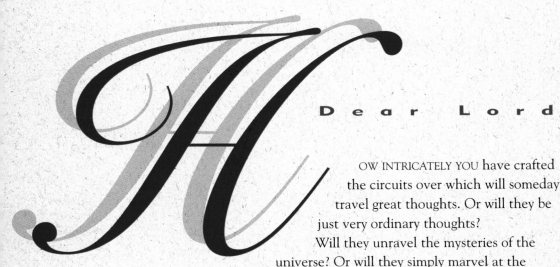

Dear Lord,

OW INTRICATELY YOU have crafted the circuits over which will someday travel great thoughts. Or will they be just very ordinary thoughts? Will they unravel the mysteries of the universe? Or will they simply marvel at the mysteries? Will they be good thoughts, thoughts of you, thoughts of others? Or will they be bad thoughts, thoughts in which she is the center of her universe, thoughts that exclude you and the worlds of other people's pain?

I pray you would watch over the thoughts that fall into those gray furrows of my child's mind. Help me, O God, to realize that the mind of this child is like a garden, which must be cultivated or else it will run wild. Enable me to plant the seeds that will someday yield a harvest of gracious words and generous deeds.

Help me to realize that though they may lie dormant now, they will take root later on. Give me a farmer's patience to wait expectantly for that day, and a farmer's persistence to keep watering and weeding until it comes. . . .

_____

_____

_____

_____

_____

_____

_____

_____

_____

_____

_____

_____

_____

_____

_____

_____

_____

_____

_____

_____

_____

_____

*L*IKE A MAJESTIC CATHEDRAL your womb is a sanctuary of sacred things, a place of hushed reverence, of dimmed light filtering through the stained glass of uterine walls, of muted hymns piped from deep within the body's organs. ❧ But the sanctuary is getting a little crowded, for now your son measures about seventeen inches and weighs a little less than three pounds. And, like a child sitting through a long sermon, your baby is starting to squirm. You may feel an elbow in your ribs, a heel on your cervix, and a head against your bladder. So it's becoming harder and harder to get comfortable, not just for you but for your baby as well.

Searching for the most comfortable position to sleep, your baby will toss and turn until he finds it. This position, or "lie", is unique to each child, and has been established as early as the fifth month. It will be the same position he will nestle into when he falls asleep in his crib.

*A*side from all the shifting around in his padded pew, something happens to break the reverent silence within your womb.

Hiccups!

Yes, hiccups. They are harmless and nothing to worry about. They are not at all uncomfortable to your baby, and, like a child squirming in church, they can provide a little entertainment—or sometimes a lot of entertainment, as they can last as long as thirty minutes.

M**other Teresa** will not allow the ferocious noises of a Calcutta street to be kept out of the chapel where she and her Sisters of Charity worship; at their prayers and receiving the Blessed Sacrament, they must still be reminded of the world, to those poorest of the poor to whom they have dedicated their lives and love.

MALCOLM MUGGERIDGE
Confessions of a Twentieth-Century Pilgrim

Dear Lord,

ORE AND MORE MY BABY is pushing his way into my world. Disrupting my sleep when he kicks. Taking away my breath when he stretches. Sending me hurrying to the bathroom when he stomps on my bladder. Sometimes the interruptions are sweet and they make me smile. Other times they are disruptive and make me wince in pain.

Help me to realize that from now on there will always be interruptions in the hushed silence of my world. Help me to realize that when this baby comes, my home will never be the same. That cathedraled quiet, that cloistered peace, will be disrupted by countless interruptions.

Help me not to shut out the noises from childhood's streets so they might become a part of my worship. Help me welcome these disruptions so they might rearrange the order of my life into a more holy liturgy—into a life that stops and listens to little voices, into a life that bends down to help little hands, into a life that reads little stories, answers little questions, dries little tears.

And, Lord, please let these noises of childhood, however distracting, however disruptive, remind me of the one to whom I have dedicated my life and my love. . . .

A Journal of My Thoughts, Feelings, and Prayers

_____

_____

_____

_____

_____

_____

_____

_____

_____

_____

_____

_____

_____

_____

_____

_____

_____

_____

_____

_____

_____

_____

_____

ABOUT SEVEN WEEKS into
your pregnancy your baby's hands and feet
started developing. In the early stages of
that development it was difficult to tell them apart as
both started out as mere buds on the arms and legs. ❧
The hands were given a day or two head start over the
feet, a seemingly insignificant advantage, yet it won't be until the third
year of your baby's life that the feet will finally catch up with them.
Then, toes digging into seashore sand will be able to keep up with fingers that are busy sculpting sand castles. ❧ After the hands and feet
began to bud, they formed digital rays, the first visible sign of the emerging

digits. Then notches between the rays developed and unfurled into webbed fingers and toes, at which point the hands could be clearly distinguished from the feet. Finally, like blossoming petals, the digits separated and became detached from each other.

The hands developed fingerprints to aid in gripping and the feet developed similar sworled ridges to give them greater traction. By week seventeen, fingernails and toenails started to grow. These nails will grow so quickly your baby will probably need a manicure soon after delivery.

When she finally does arrive, she will bring all her own toys: hands to "patty-cake" with, fingers to wiggle; toes to play "this-little-piggy" with, feet to tickle. These toys will keep her occupied for hours on end as she plays in her crib. But she won't be selfish with them; she will delight in sharing her toys so you can play too.

> **A** wife
> of noble character who
> can find?...
> In her hand she holds
> the distaff and grasps
> the spindle with
> her fingers.
> She opens her arms to
> the poor and extends
> her hands to the needy.
> ... Her children arise
> and call her blessed.
>
>
>
> PROVERBS
> 31:10,19–20,28

T

Dear Lord,

PRAY FOR MY BABY'S FEET. Help them turn from the deceptive paths that lead to destruction, as well as the well-traveled paths that lead to conformity. With the lamp of your Word to light her path, show her the way you would have those feet to travel. Give her the clarity she needs to see that path and the courage she needs to walk it, especially at those times she has to walk it alone.

And as she walks that path, Lord, give her feet that are always quick to come to the aid of anyone along that path who is in need. Give her hands that extend themselves to those whose lives are less fortunate than her own. May they be open to the hungry and the homeless, to the poor and the thirsty, to those who are out-of-work and weary and wondering if anybody really cares.

Help me to realize, Lord, that my child will do what she sees me doing; her feet will walk where mine walk, her hands will do what mine do.

I confess that I often get so busy with my work that I overlook those who have no work to do, who have no home to clean or meals to cook or dishes to wash.

Help me to realize, Lord, that the woman of Proverbs 31 was a woman who was busy with her work yet was never too busy to extend her hands to the poor and needy. And help me also realize that this was one of the things her children not only remembered her for but blessed her for. . . .

A Journal of My Thoughts, Feelings, and Prayers

*I*N ONLY THIRTY-ONE WEEKS your baby has gone from a barely visible seed to a slender trunk branching with arms, legs, and a head. From the tip of that head to the bottom of his feet your baby measures nineteen inches. ❧ He fits so snugly in your womb that he can no longer do the somersaults and back flips he once could. The most acrobatic he will get will be to stand on his head. As the head is the heaviest part of his body, this position is most comfortable for your baby. And, it is also the best position to get ready for his upcoming journey through the birth canal. ❧ From this inverted position your baby will still exercise, but it will be limited to turning from side to side. You will feel his hands trace across your abdomen, almost as if he is feeling around in the dark for a doorknob to get him out of the cramped closet he is now in. Sometimes the baby will get into a tucked position, pulling his knees up to his nose. On occasion, he may even let fly a swift kick, a kick so hard it can knock a book off your lap.

Your insides feel displaced, and you're probably thinking there's no room for your baby to grow. And yet he only weighs around three-and-a-half pounds. Which means he will double in size in the next two-and-a-half months.

By then, your baby will be like a potted plant desperately needing to be transplanted and straining at your insides for room to grow.

> Scratch
> the green
> rind of a sapling,
> or wantonly twist it
> in the soil,
> and a scarred
> or crooked oak
> will tell of the act
> for centuries to come.
> So it is with
> the teaching of youth,
> which makes
> impressions on the
> mind and heart that
> are to last
> forever.
>
>
>
> SOURCE UNKNOWN

Dear Lord,

E STARTED GROWING within me so quietly, so unobtrusively. Just a tiny little seed. And yet now he is growing so fast that sometimes I feel I might burst. In a couple of months he will out-grow me, Lord. Prepare my heart for that not-too-distant day. And prepare my home so it might provide the fertile soil he will need to grow.

Thank you so much for entrusting this tenderly budding life to my care. Keep me from disciplining him too severely, from pruning back his eager leaves in their skyward stretch for the sun.

Help me to realize how fragile this little child is, how tentative are his roots, how windblown are his moods. Help me to realize that the rind surrounding him is green and tender, and that the wounds inflicted in childhood will form the scars he may carry with him the rest of his life.

There will be times, I know, when this little boy will exasperate me. When he tracks mud across my freshly waxed floor. When he roughhouses in the living room and breaks a lamp. When he gets sassy and talks back. Or when he gets pouty and huffs off while I'm talking to him. At those times, Lord, give me an added measure of your grace so I may have the wisdom and the restraint I need to deal with the situation in a way that would not scar him.

Help me to respect the way he is inclined to grow, sensitive both to his talents and to his temperament. Help me to nurture him as a gardener would a young sapling, allowing it to grow according to its natural inclinations so its unique beauty can be shared with the world. . . .

A Journal of My Thoughts, Feelings, and Prayers

THIS LAST TRIMESTER will be the most exhausting part of your pregnancy. Besides the additional weight you are carrying, there's little relief when you get off your feet. No matter how you contort yourself you can't seem to find a comfortable position to sleep in. You can't stretch out on your back or lie on your stomach. All you can do is sleep on your side, propped with pillows—pillows between your thighs, under your head, behind your back, next to your stomach—but still you can't get comfortable. The baby is either stretching or kicking or trying to get comfortable herself. Your bladder gets you up several times during the night. And when you finally do drift off to sleep, it never seems deep enough or long enough. Part of that reason is be-cause of your dreams.

Some of the time those brief interludes of rest bring with them the most heartwarming of dreams; other times, they bring the most heartrending of nightmares—terrifying scenes of misplacing your baby and forgetting where you left her, of acciden-tally dropping your baby, of her getting sick or even dying.

As disturbing as these dreams are, they shouldn't be dismissed, because they mirror your subcon-scious, reflecting your fears and anxieties.

As you sleep, those fears slip from your subcon-scious and articulate themselves in very real, very emotional dreams. Far from being an unhealthy sign, these dreams indicate how concerned you are about your baby's health and how concerned you are about being a good mother. And far from being destructive, even the most unsettling of dreams can be turned into the most reassuring of prayers.

> Do not be anxious about anything, but in everything, by prayer and petition, with thanksgiving, present your requests to God. And the peace of God, which transcends all un-derstanding, will guard your hearts and minds in Christ Jesus.
>
>
>
> PHILIPPIANS 4:6–7

Dear Lord,

'VE BEEN SO TIRED LATELY. I can't get comfortable when I lie down, and just when I'm able to prop myself with pillows and get halfway comfortable, I have to get up to use the bathroom. And when I do finally drift off to sleep, I don't get much rest. Either the baby kicks me awake or else it's the nightmares. Sometimes they seem so real, Lord. They jolt me awake at night and haunt me all the next day. Where do those dreams come from? Deep down in my subconscious, do I fear all those things happening? What is it I'm afraid of? Show me, Lord. Bring my fears out in the open. Identify them for me so I can turn my fears into opportunities to trust you.

Lord, when I wake up in the middle of the night with a bad dream, give me the resolve to turn that nightmare into a prayer. And the next day, give me the grace to turn any residual anxiety into a peace that transcends all understanding. Use that peace to guard my heart and mind, watching like a sentry to make sure no more anxious thoughts sneak in through my subconscious.

Help me, Lord, please. I want to spend these next two months in anticipation of this baby's arrival, not in anxiety over all the things that could go wrong. I want to use my time, even my sleepless time, productively, folding my hands in prayer, not wringing them in worry. . . .

𝒴OUR BABY IS WEIGHING close to four-and-a-half pounds now. With the due date just around the corner and approaching fast, you may experience some anxiety about giving birth. ❧ Will the pain be too much? Will I scream? Will I lose control of my bladder and embarrass myself? Will I need a C-section? ❧ These feelings are completely natural. It's also natural to have some fairly severe bouts with depression. This isn't an emotional or spiritual problem; it's simply hormonal. During your normal menstrual cycle you produce a few milligrams a day of the key hormone progesterone. During the end of your pregnancy you produce nearly 250 milligrams a day. While the progesterone output multiplies by 50–60 times, the output of another important hormone, estrogen, multiplies by 20–30 times. ❧ So don't be surprised if sudden waves of emotion come sweeping over you without warning. You'll get down in the dumps. You'll cry for no reason.

3

You'll think you're unfit to be a mother. And sometimes, when the hormonal storm gets really rough,
you'll think you're going to drown in a sea of despair.

But just like any other storms, those feelings will
pass. The clouds of depression will move off the
horizon, and you'll be back to your old sunny self
again.

Another thing that may cause you some concern
is the sporadic contractions you've been having. Is
this normal? Is something wrong with the baby? Am
I going to deliver prematurely?

What you are probably experiencing are Braxton Hicks contractions. These
contractions are the uterus's way of warming up for the main event that will
take place in another six weeks or so. They can last from thirty seconds to two
minutes and give you a pretty good scare if you're not prepared for them.

Starting at the top of the uterus and moving downward, the contractions
will feel as if the muscles are knotting up.

Despite how intense they feel, these contractions are not strong enough to
deliver your baby. Just look at them as God's way of tapping you on the shoulder
to make sure your bags are packed and to ease some of the anxiety about the job
ahead of you.

It will be hard work. Probably the hardest work you will ever do. But you'll
be able to do it. You'll have plenty of help in the delivery room and plenty of
people on the sidelines rooting for you.

> **As
> a mother
> comforts her child,
> so I will
> comfort you.**
>
> ISAIAH 66:13

Dear Lord,

HANK YOU FOR ALL the maternal instincts you
have given me, for how natural it is for me to want
to comfort my child. When he cries in the middle of
the night, I will wake up and go to him. When he is wet,
I will change him. When he is hungry, I will feed him. When
he is frightened, I will rock him in my arms.

I will be there for him because he is my child. And because he needs me.

Wherever he needs me, whenever he needs me, however he needs me, I will
be there. I will be there in the bathroom to help him take a bath, and in the
backyard to help him climb a tree. I will be there with a bedtime story when he
lies down at night, and with breakfast when he wakes up in the morning. I will
be there to glue a broken toy or to blot a bloody nose.

I will be there for him because he is my child. And because he needs me.

I know, Lord, that if I have all those feelings for my child, how much greater
must be the feelings you have for yours. If I am willing to do all those things to
comfort my little one, how much greater must be your willingness to comfort
the little ones who belong to you.

Thank you, Lord, that you have promised to be there for me simply because
I am your child. And because I need you.

I need you now, Lord, to come to me in my depression and to hold me until
my hormones subside. . . .

A Journal of My Thoughts, Feelings, and Prayers

_____

_____

_____

_____

_____

_____

_____

_____

_____

_____

_____

_____

_____

_____

_____

_____

_____

_____

_____

_____

_____

_____

OUR BABY weighs almost five pounds now and is just under twenty inches long. Her lungs have been developing since about the fourth month, and, with the exception of the air sacs, are now mature enough to breathe the air outside the womb. Since the respiratory system is the last thing to develop, a baby entering the world too prematurely could develop respiratory distress syndrome and have difficulty breathing on its own. In cases like this, oxygen and breathing machines called ventilators may be necessary until the lungs mature.

4

Presently, your baby's lungs are bathed in amniotic fluid in a completely airless environment. Despite that fact, your baby's lungs have been inhaling and exhaling for many months now. Such rehearsal is crucial to strengthen the lungs for that first big breath at birth.

Even with practice, that first breath will be a hard one for your baby, five times more difficult than an ordinary breath. It will be something like blowing up a balloon for the first time, for that breath must inflate thousands of tiny air sacs in the lungs which have never before been inflated. That is why those early cries are so important. Besides inflating the lungs, they help clear mucus from the air sacs and bronchial passages so more air can enter.

Gradually, breathing will become easier for your baby, but for the first few days it will be a little halting and irregular.

> **P**rayer should be as natural as breathing and as necessary as oxygen.
>
>
>
> EDITH SCHAEFFER
> *Common Sense Living*

Dear Lord,

I HAVE BEEN PRAYING for this baby for a long time now. As I think about her developing lungs, I am reminded how natural and how necessary prayer should be in my life.

Give me that type of ease when I pray, Lord, like the involuntary inhaling and exhaling of air. Give me that type of urgency so I may understand how desperately I need it to sustain my spiritual life.

Every time I tiptoe into the nursery and watch my baby sleeping, her little chest moving up and down so effortlessly, sweetly remind me of these many times I have prayed for her.

Remind me, too, that my little girl will always need her mother's prayers. Prayers to help her understand the death of a pet . . . or a grandparent. Prayers to help her get along with a playmate . . . or to get her through the first day of school. Prayers to mend a boo-boo . . . or a broken heart.

*H*elp me to realize, Lord, that I have only begun to pray. A whole life stretches before her. I know I will not always be able to go with her, not always be there to hold her hand or point the way or pick her up when she falls. But comfort me in the fact that though I will not always be able to go with her, my prayers will. . . .

A Journal of My Thoughts, Feelings, and Prayers

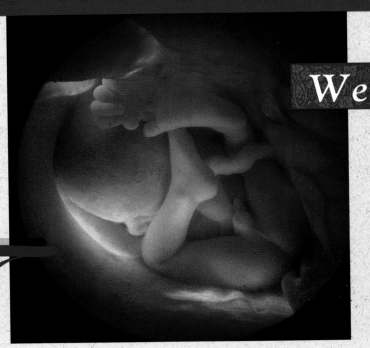

THE FRUIT OF YOUR WOMB ripens within you only because of the vine it is attached to—the umbilical cord. This cord connects the baby to the placenta that is rooted in your uterus. This milky-colored cord is made up of three inter-twined blood vessels: two smaller arteries carry used blood from the baby to the placenta; the larger vein brings nutrient-rich, oxygenated blood to the baby. ❧ These blood vessels are embed-ded in a gelatinous substance known as Wharton's jelly and encased in a membrane like a sausage-skin that holds them all together. Your baby's heart beats twice as fast as yours, pumping blood through

5

these vessels at a speed of about four miles per hour, completing a round trip through the baby in only thirty seconds. This constant flow of blood keeps the cord distended and, along with the Wharton's jelly, keeps it from getting knotted or tangled. If it weren't for the way the umbilical cord was designed, the blood supply could easily become crimped or cut off completely when the cord gets twisted. Once inside the body, the blood travels to the fetal heart where it is pumped to the brain and to the rest of the body. Since the lungs have not yet expanded and are unable to produce oxygen, they are by-passed. But at birth a small miracle occurs with those lungs, without which your baby could not survive the abrupt and radical change of environment. At birth the blood vessels around the baby's navel automatically seal themselves off, halting the flow of blood from the umbilical cord. Simultaneously, an opening between the atria closes, shunting blood into the previously bypassed lungs, which will immediately assume the work of oxygenation.

The roots of the placenta, the vine of the umbilical cord, and the fruit of your womb are all growing within the well-irrigated vineyard of your uterus. Together they picture how essential is the bond linking baby and mother together.

> I am the vine; you are the branches. If a man remains in me and I in him, he will bear much fruit; apart from me you can do nothing.
>
>
>
> JOHN 15:5

Dear Lord,

OW VITAL IS THIS DELICATE VINE that links the two of us together, him to me and me to him. Thank you how it nourishes him, cleanses him, and keeps him healthy and growing, for without it he would wither and die.

Thank you for the picture of dependence that the umbilical cord reveals. How vital is my fellowship with you, Lord; how it nourishes me, cleanses me, keeps me healthy and growing.

Help me to realize that apart from you I can do nothing. Apart from your life flowing through mine, I can at best only produce artificial fruit. It may look good, but it doesn't nourish, and it doesn't last, and it doesn't have the seeds to reproduce itself. And with a world starving for spiritual reality, what good is that? Except for looks.

I don't want to look fruitful, Lord; I want to *be* fruitful. And I want my child to be fruitful too.

I want his relationship with you to be vital. Help him to grow up trusting you to be the lifeline to his spiritual life. Drawing from you his nourishment. Giving to you his life for cleansing. Growing. Blossoming. And in due season, bearing fruit of his own. . . .

A Journal of My Thoughts, Feelings, and Prayers

URING the last four or five weeks of pregnancy your baby will be gaining around an ounce a day. You probably, and quite understandably, have some apprehensions about how your little one will fare coming into a drafty world. After all, babies are so delicate. ⊱ But your baby has been well-prepared for the world she is about to enter. Over the past month she has gained a significant amount of fat. Besides being the place where some of the essential vitamins like A and D are stored, this layer of fat also serves as a thermal blanket. That is one reason why premature babies are kept in incubators; they don't have enough fat on their bodies to keep themselves warm. ⊱ But what about the threat of illness and disease? After all, the world she is entering is not only drafty but filled with germs.

Over the years you have developed immunities to certain types of diseases such as measles, mumps, whooping cough, and chicken pox. These immunities are resident within your blood in the form of disease-fighting proteins called antibodies. Through the course of the pregnancy, most particularly over the past three months, these antibodies were passed on to your child.

To further protect your newborn, antibodies will be transmitted through your breast milk, along with a rich supply of vitamins and minerals. These antibodies are especially concentrated in the colostrum, the watery fluid your baby will take from your breast until your milk comes in, a day or two after delivery.

Already your body is preparing for that event. Your very bones have softened and the ligaments in your back have loosened to make an easier passage for your baby. Your cervix has also begun to soften and thin, a process known as effacing, and when its mucus plug comes out, you'll know that the countdown to delivery has begun.

> See to it that you do not look down on one of these little ones. For I tell you that their angels in heaven always see the face of my Father in heaven.
>
>
>
> MATTHEW 18:10–11

Dear Lord,

HANK YOU FOR THE PROVISIONS you have made to make sure my baby is safe and warm when she arrives into this world. Thank you for the layer of fat that blankets her, and for the antibodies that protect her.

Thank you for the bones that will soften, the ligaments that will loosen, the cervix that will dilate, to enable her to endure the difficult journey of childbirth.

You have taken such good care of her, Lord. And I know that after she is born, you will continue to protect her and to help her as she journeys on her way to growing up.

Thank you for the angel you have provided to watch over her along that journey. And thank you that it is no menial angel but an angel who has continual access to you, who stands before you and talks with you.

Tell that angel how honored I feel to have him watching over my child. Thank him for me, Lord. Thank him for being there when I am not. For being diligent when I cannot. For being strong on behalf of someone so weak. For being a force for good in a world that lies in the power of the evil one. For all that he will do that I will never know, thank him for me—thank him from the bottom of a mother's heart. . . .

A Journal of My Thoughts, Feelings, and Prayers

_____

_____

_____

_____

_____

_____

_____

_____

_____

_____

_____

_____

_____

_____

_____

_____

_____

_____

_____

_____

_____

_____

_____

_____

_____

_____

OUR BABY is now about six-and-a-half pounds and stands twenty-one inches tall. You're probably feeling as though you swallowed the Thanksgiving turkey and don't have room for even a sliver of pie. Fortunately, relief is just around the corner. ❧ Most women get a little relief when their baby descends or "drops" into the pelvic area. This often tilts your belly a bit forward and lowers the uterus a couple of inches. ❧ The good news is, you'll have room for that slice of pumpkin pie and a generous daub of whipped cream. The bad news is, you'll have to use the bathroom more often because the shift in weight puts more pressure on your bladder.

Once your baby has dropped, the head positions itself into the birth canal, the upper boundary of the pelvis. This will restrict your baby's movement considerably, although you will be able to feel him rotating his head.

The discomfort you have felt thus far in your pregnancy will shift as your weight shifts. In some cases it will be alleviated; in others, exacerbated. For example, you will be able to breathe easier, but you will probably experience sharp, sudden pains in your pelvis that you have not felt before now.

Like an arrow placed in position on a bowstring, your baby is now engaged and ready to be sent forth into the world.

Y ou are the bows from which your children as living arrows are sent forth.

The archer sees the mark upon the path of the infinite, and He bends you with His might that His arrows may go swift and far.

Let your bending in the archer's hand be for gladness.

For even as He loves the arrow that flies, so He loves also the bow that is stable.

KAHLIL GIBRAN
The Prophet

Dear Lord,

THANK YOU for this little arrow of mine that is now in position to be sent forth into the world. Help me to set my sights on the right target, aiming him so he would make a mark on eternity. May he travel straight and true, swift and far. And for those times he veers off course or falls short of your glory, please forgive him.

Thank you, Lord, that you not only love the arrow that flies but also the bow that is stable. Help me to be steady in my aim. Help me to be firm yet flexible, realizing that the strength of the bow lies not in its rigidity but in its ability to bend.

Keep me from breaking, Lord, for often I am prone to set my sights too high and pull back the bow too hard.

Let my bending be for gladness, both in childbirth and in child rearing. Let me delight in launching this little child into the world. And let me delight in all the launchings that will follow: in sending him off for the first day of school, in sending him off for college, in sending him off to a career, and in sending him off in marriage to make a life of his own.

When those times come, give me the strength not only to bend the bow but the strength to release the arrow, for that will be the hardest part of all. . . .

*Y*OUR BABY weighs around seven pounds, and growth has all but stopped now, so, with the exception of her lungs, your baby won't change much. ❧ But, oh, how this baby has changed you. ❧ During pregnancy the volume of blood circulating within you has increased by 45 percent to meet the added demands that the uterus requires. Since there's more blood, that means your heart has to work harder to pump it. It enlarges to meet the demand and increases its pulse rate by ten to fifteen beats per minute. That is why your skin is warmer, pinker, and sweats more. ❧ The more blood there is, the more oxygen it needs and the more waste products it needs to dispose of, which means extra work for the lungs and kidneys. Which helps explain why you have had to go to the bathroom so much and why you have been so tired. ❧ Along with those changes come changes in the skin. Your skin may have darkened a shade or two, and the pigmentation around the nipples and areolas has also darkened. A dark, vertical line called the linea nigra formed down the middle of your abdomen. Often, too, the skin develops stretch marks.

You likely have lost a noticeable amount of hair, and what you have has probably become greasy due to high levels of progesterone in the blood, which stimulate the oil glands on your scalp. Your gums have become softer and your teeth, more susceptible to decay.

Aside from all these physical changes are changes in your emotions from the flood of hormones that are released. That tide of hormones caused an ebb and flow of your emotions, resulting in anxiety, self-esteem problems, and buckets of unexplained tears. But you will get your hair back in time. The linea nigra will fade and eventually disappear. Your hormones will get back to normal levels, and you'll probably fit into your old clothes again. But one thing will never go back to the way it was.

You.

*Y*ou look at the world differently now. You look at life differently, and yourself differently.

Your baby has changed you—forever—and, by the grace of God, she will continue to do so all of your life.

"What is REAL?" asked the Rabbit one day. "Does it mean having things that buzz inside you and a stick-out handle?"

"Real isn't how you are made," said the Skin Horse. "It's a thing that happens to you. When a child loves you for a long, long time, not just to play with, but REALLY loves you, then you become Real."

"Does it hurt?"

"Sometimes." For he was always truthful. "When you are Real you don't mind being hurt."

"Does it happen all at once, like being wound up, or bit by bit?"

"It doesn't happen all at once. You become. It takes a long time. That's why it doesn't happen to people who break easily, or who have sharp edges, or who have to be carefully kept. Generally, by the time you are Real most of your hair has been loved off, and your eyes drop out and you get loose in the joints and very shabby."

MARGERY WILLIAMS
The Velveteen Rabbit

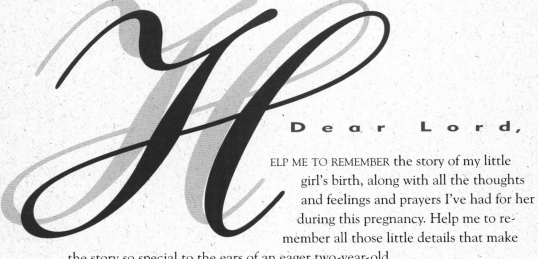

HELP ME TO REMEMBER the story of my little girl's birth, along with all the thoughts and feelings and prayers I've had for her during this pregnancy. Help me to remember all those little details that make the story so special to the ears of an eager two-year-old.

Thank you that after this baby is born my body will get back to normal. Thank you that I will be able to regain my dress size as well as my sanity. I can't wait to walk up a flight of stairs without getting winded, or eat a big meal without getting heartburn, or to sleep on my stomach again.

But I'm glad there will be some things that won't go back to the way they were. Like me.

I will never be the same. And I think that is a good thing.

Keep the changes coming, Lord. Keep me from being a mother who breaks easily or who has sharp edges and has to be carefully kept. Help me to be soft and huggable and not so worried about getting my hands dirty or my clothes wrinkled or getting cookie dough in my hair.

Help me to realize that if ever I am to become a real human being— vulnerable and caring and kind—it will be due in large measure to the longtime love of a child.

I know she will love me when there's cookies and milk and a mother's lap where stories are read. Help her to love me when she's too big to sit on my lap and I'm too blind to read her stories. For someday I will be old and shabby and loose in the joints. And then I will need her love more than ever. . . .

A Journal of My Thoughts, Feelings, and Prayers ❧

*L*ABOR MAY last anywhere from one hour to a marathon of hours. The average is about eight, unless it's your first baby, in which case the average is about fourteen. You will know you are in labor when your contractions grow stronger and closer together. ❧ About fifteen percent of women are notified early that their baby is on the way. The notice comes when the amniotic sac ruptures, something referred to as "your water breaking." You may feel an embarrassing gush of warm water if you're lying down. If you're standing up when it happens, you'll probably just feel a trickle, as the baby's head acts as a cork to seal off much of the leakage. ❧ Though science is not exactly sure what triggers labor, it may happen in response to the lack of space in the uterus and the diminishing ability of the placenta to provide nourishment. This danger signal may trigger a chemical from the fetal brain to stimulate the uterus to contract. ❧ In the early phase of labor the contractions will be so slight you may not even notice them. By the end of this phase, however, they will become significantly stronger, at which time your cervix will begin to dilate.

At the hospital, your cervix will continue to dilate to seven centimeters during the next phase, known as active labor. During this time your contractions and your baby's heart rate will be carefully monitored. The contractions will now grow stronger and closer together.

Beginning like a faint humming in the tracks around your uterus, the contractions will seem like the distant rumble of railroad cars coming closer and closer until suddenly the contraction will be upon you. The ground will quake as it goes clattering by, and it will occupy your entire attention. Then, as quickly as it came, it will go humming away down the tracks and be gone.

> **D**o not fear, for I am with you; do not be dismayed, for I am your God.
>
> I will strengthen you and help you;
>
> I will uphold you with my righteous right hand.
>
>
>
> ISAIAH 41:10

With each contraction the muscles at the top of your uterus will exert fifty pounds of pressure, compressing the placenta and the umbilical cord, which very briefly reduces the oxygen supply to your baby. During a strong contraction your baby's pulse will slow, but when the contraction subsides, it will return to normal.

As painful as they are, these contractions are merely the warm-up for the even harder transition and pushing phase of your labor. In that phase, each contraction will require greater concentration and strength as you work with your uterus to push your baby through the birth canal.

It is natural to be afraid during labor, especially if it's your first time or if you've had a bad experience with your labor in the past. Many women prefer to have an anesthetic to reduce the pain of childbirth, and there will be an anesthesiologist on hand in case you need one.

So remember, all the help you need to get you through your labor will be available to you—both human and divine.

P Dear Lord,

LEASE BE WITH ME IN MY LABOR. I am frightened for
how painful it will be, frightened I won't be strong
enough, that something could go wrong. Hold my hand,
Lord, and help me get though this.

Be with my baby, too. It will be a difficult journey for him as well. Thank you
for all the provisions you've made to ensure that he will get the oxygen he needs
for his journey. Keep him safe and from being too scared.

Be with my husband, Lord. It will be hard work for him as well. A different
kind of hard. A more emotional kind. May this birthing experience bring us
closer together, bond us as a couple, as family.

May it be a holy experience for him as it will be for me. He hasn't felt all the
things I've felt from carrying this baby inside me for the last nine months. And
he hasn't been able to enter into all the wonderful things I have experienced.
Open the curtain, Lord, on this most holy experience and let him see some
of the glory.

Give me the strength I need for the work that lies ahead. And for my doctor
and for the nurses who will assist in the delivery, be with them too, for in a very
real sense, they will be in labor with me. . . .

A Journal of My Thoughts, Feelings, and Prayers

WHEN YOUR CERVIX has completely
dilated, the contractions will be the hardest
they've been, inching your baby through
the birth canal. With every contraction you will alternate panting and pushing. Your hair will blot the pin-
heads of sweat that collect on your scalp. Your mouth
will be parched, but the best you can hope for is an ice chip to suck on.
After each contraction you'll try to catch your breath, but almost as
soon as the last wave of pain washes away, another will crest and come
crashing over you. Finally, with an excruciating push, the baby's
head will crown. The combined pressure of the contractions and your
pushing now exerts nearly one hundred pounds of pressure on your
baby. If that isn't enough to push her head through the vaginal opening, the doctor will perform an episiotomy, an incision at the lower end
of that opening, which prevents the baby's head from raggedly tearing
your flesh. When your baby's slippery head finally does pop out, it
will be a moment of triumph . . . and relief. The head will be wrinkled

and misshapen from the constricting tunnel it has been pushed through. With another push or two your baby's shoulders will squeeze out. Then, with a final push, she'll slip into the world, mottled bluish-gray and looking as if she were slathered with grease.

When your baby gives her first slurpy cry, the doctor will be there to suction out the obstructing liquid from her mouth, nostrils, and ears. As soon as the first breath is taken, the skin will begin looking healthier. As sudden as a blush, the blues and grays will turn pink. If you are dark-skinned, it may take several days, even weeks, for the pigments to surface in your baby's skin.

The nurses will wipe your baby down, take her temperature, put antibiotic liquid in her eyes, and apply an antiseptic solution on the place where the umbilical cord was cut. Then they'll put a hospital I.D. bracelet around your baby's foot and hand and take her footprint.

These will be strange, new, and somewhat frightening sensations for your baby. Already she has endured the disorienting experience of being evicted from your womb. Now there are bright lights, a sudden discord of sounds, and all sorts of strange sensations brushing against her body.

Her helpless cries and her shivering lips will call out for you. When you answer, it will be the first familiar sound your baby hears. When she is placed on your chest and feels the warmth of your flesh and the familiar rhythms of your heart, she will instinctively recognize you, the mother she has waited these so many months to meet.

> A woman giving birth to a child has pain because her time has come; but when her baby is born she forgets the anguish because of her joy that a child is born into the world.
>
> JOHN 16:21

Dear Lord,

'M READY NOW, ready to go to the hospital and have this baby. I know it will be hard, but I'm ready for that too. For I know you will be there with me. Holding my hand. Helping me. Pushing with me to bring this baby into the world.

When this baby does come into the world, Lord, I want you to know that I dedicate her to you.

Thank you for how you've prepared me for the birth of this child. Thank you for all the instruction I've received from my doctor. For all the encouragement I've received from my family. For all the advice I've received from my friends. And thank you for all the remarkable ways my body has readied itself for this moment.

I know there will be pain. But there will also be joy. And the joy will be greater than the pain.

Help me through my labor, Lord, especially through the pain of transition.

Thank you for allowing me to be the mother of this miracle, this slow miracle of life that has been ripening within me for the past nine months. Thank you for giving me so much time to prepare for this day. I think I needed it as much as my baby did.

She's ready now, Lord.

And I'm ready now, too. . . .

NAME

BIRTHDATE

PLACE OF BIRTH

THE DELIVERING DOCTOR

HEIGHT

WEIGHT

Photogragh

we are your everything
when your daddy cut the cord it was only the beginning of dependency
for from our hearts you will take all you need
and the best we can give you is Jesus

the best we can show you is His love
so that one day all you need will come from His heart and
He will be your everything.

JULIE MARTIN
A Time To Be Born

A Letter Welcoming My Baby into the World